T0285542

THE ART OF THE
TURNAROUND

THE ART OF THE
TURNAROUND

A Comprehensive 10-Step Guide

Mike Dunlop

**BARLOW
BOOKS**

Library and Archives Canada Cataloguing in Publication data available upon request.

978-1-998841-15-8 (hardcover)

Printed in Canada

Publisher: Sarah Scott
Book producer: Tracy Bordian/At Large Editorial Services
Cover design: Paul Hodgson
Interior design and layout: Ruth Dwight
Copy editing: Eleanor Gasparik
Indexing: Rhiannon Thomas

For more information, visit **www.barlowbooks.com**

Barlow Book Publishing Inc.
96 Elm Avenue, Toronto, ON
M4W 1P2 Canada

*For everyone who helped me along
this wonderful journey*

CONTENTS

INTRODUCTION

Without much warning, here I was in Belgium, decamped from the United States to start my first overseas turnaround. My first thought was a paraphrase of the famous Laurel and Hardy quote, "Well, here's a fine mess I have got myself into." The company, Technical Airborne Components Industries (TAC), was owned by Fabrique Nationale, a major arms manufacturer in Belgium. TAC had not made a profit in its nine-year existence, so the parent company was enthusiastic about getting rid of it. I had negotiated an attractive price to buy the company but now I was faced with the realization that I was on my own, with a very modest command of the French language to support me. Three languages were spoken in the company: French, Spanish, and Flemish. I decided my only lifeboat language was French so I enrolled in a course called *Immersion totale* (total immersion). After four weeks I was not totally reliant on my translator, who I found out later was not exactly translating what I was saying or correctly translating the replies. My challenges included having two unions, one representing French- and Spanish-speaking (Catholic) employees and the other representing Dutch-speaking (Protestant) employees. Jet-lagged and completely isolated, I was now in the turn-around Olympics of my life with only one medal available, a "win." As you will find out when reading this book, even the most challenging company can be turned around. It may be trite to say it, but the darkest hour is always before dawn in the turnaround process.

MY FIRST COMPANY turnaround came about by accident. I had just been unceremoniously fired from my first job in the United States after emigrating to Seattle from England earlier that year. My job, with a division of a major US conglomerate called Litton Industries, was to sell and install job-cost software for the construction industry. It was obvious early on in my sales career that the software had major deficiencies that made it unsaleable and unusable. In 1973 we did not have email, so the only way of communicating effectively with the head office in Newark, New Jersey, was by mail. My numerous letters outlining the deficiencies and asking for help were completely ignored. Without these major changes I felt like I had been left on a raft without a paddle. The US was facing the worst recession since World War II, so even though the idea of finding a new job crossed my mind, it would have been exceedingly difficult. I decided that rewriting sections of the software to make it saleable was the lowest-risk option. What I had not anticipated was how successful my software changes would be, and I rapidly vaulted into the top ranks of Litton Industries's salespeople in the US. That unfortunately got me notoriety and attention that I was not looking for. I was summoned to Newark to explain my successful sales campaign. There was no alternative but to fess up. This led to an impromptu meeting with the CEO and their general counsel. As luck would have it, a simple question saved me. The general counsel wanted to know whether I wrote the software on my time or the company time. Without realizing the importance of the question, I answered honestly. I emphatically told him, "On my own time of course." This answer led to further discussions and a decision to pay me for my enhancements because they intended to incorporate them into their own software. I don't know whether or not they were generous, but the payment was more money than I had ever seen in my life.

Before my departure I was asked to meet with the CEO for a second and final time. He told me that in the future there was no way I would be able to work in a corporate environment. He told me I needed to work for myself and then I could choose whatever I wanted to do and make any changes I thought appropriate. What he described made me realize that I was free to set my own path. This advice and encouragement changed my life and provided me with the foundation for an exciting and fulfilling fifty-plus years of working in various entrepreneurial endeavors.

The first company I founded was called Computer Information Center. It was a full turnkey service for businesses that were planning to purchase their first computers. This was the early 1970s, a time when many small- to medium-sized companies did not have computers and had no idea how to choose the right one for their business or choose appropriate software. The unique service I offered was to select the best computer for their needs, select the software that would work in their industry, and complete a full system implementation including training. No other company was offering a service like this at the time. Charging a fair fixed fee meant the customer would know exactly how much they were going to spend. Seattle had a small business community so the referral base grew rapidly, and I soon had a thriving business. What I did not realize was that this business would morph into a new opportunity that, with the help of a wonderful mentor, would keep me focused for many years. The new business was helping companies in financial difficulties. The opportunity to ply my skills in complex puzzle solving suddenly became a reality.

My first turnaround presented itself while I was implementing a computer system for a major Seattle retail jewelry chain. It was clear that the family-owned company was facing significant business and financial challenges, like many companies were at the time. I did not need to do any sophisticated forensic accounting to know this. Simply overhearing the employees talk about the suppliers who were threatening to stop shipments because they were not being paid gave me a clue that there was trouble in Dodge City. This became even more obvious when I was installing their financial reporting system. Even to my inexperienced eye, I could see that their liabilities exceeded the true value of their assets. The technical term for this is insolvency, which is normally the precursor to bankruptcy.

My initial reaction was alarm — that I was not going to get paid for my computer services. But once I calmed my nerves, it was obvious to me that there were many improvements the company could make to remedy their difficulties. I started making notes on everything that I felt could help them. I also decided to present my findings to the family patriarch and see how he was going to address the impending financial doom. It turned out that the company's demise was going to happen sooner than I expected: late on a Friday night he told me that there was a high probability they would have to cease operations. Partly out of self-preservation and partly because I wanted to help, I told him there were numerous opportunities to improve his company's profitability and I would be happy to go over them with him. He told me he had a meeting with a senior bank officer at ten o'clock on Monday morning and immediately asked if I wouldn't mind putting together my suggestions into a business plan over the weekend and delivering it to him before his bank meeting.

Over that weekend I set out to create a recovery plan. Some of the items were obvious but many were a little bit more nuanced. One item that could bring immediate financial relief was selling the accounts receivable to get immediate cash for all sales rather than have to bill customers and wait for payment. This was before the mass use of credit cards and was a common practice with many retailers (it is also known as factoring). This would immediately turn the business into a cash business and a third party would be responsible for collecting the money. The practice of allowing customers to have their own account was a throwback to earlier times when wealthy people rarely dealt in cash. There was also a practical reason why this archaic system was used. Some of the more well-known customers had two accounts, one where the bill was sent to their home address and the other where it went to their office to avoid scrutiny of prying domestic eyes. The office bills were always significantly larger than the domestic ones.

After working all weekend and delivering the plan to the owner as promised, I did not expect to hear from him for a while. The plan included closing some of the very unprofitable stores, reducing inventory in the stores, and reviewing pricing to make sure of sufficient margin. The headquarters of the company also seemed to be summer camp for relatives, so additional changes were made to reduce the cost of the headquarters.

I was surprised to receive a call from the owner so soon after his meeting with the bank. He asked me if I could join him right then at the bank. I was convinced that he had bad news for me. It was the opposite. The wonderful banker he was dealing with had requested an immediate meeting with the person who had put the business plan together—me! His name was Dave Friedenberg, and he quickly introduced himself as the head of commercial lending for the largest bank in the area, Seattle First National Bank. Dave was blunt and direct: if the owner would retain me to implement the recovery plan, he would not only renew the existing credit line but extend the company additional credit if needed. The owner of the business agreed at once, and suddenly, at the age of twenty-seven, I had morphed seamlessly into a business consultant. The turnaround was rapid, with many changes being implemented almost immediately, including many that I've outlined in this book. I learned to ignore the frequent entreaties from the owner that I was making too many changes and making them too quickly. I had the advantage of knowing that I held the ultimate trump card: the owner's fear of facing his banker Dave Friedenberg again.

The financial results improved rapidly and it became obvious to the bank that the company's need for credit had reduced dramatically.

A METHOD PROVEN OVER DECADES

That serendipitous meeting with David Friedenberg turned into a seventeen-year partnership, during which I helped turn around thirty-four companies that were in various stages of financial demise. After seeing my turnaround work with the jewelry company, David introduced me to all the loan officers at his bank to work with companies that were having financial difficulties. This gave me not only steady work but also immense enjoyment in the renovation of companies that were headed for oblivion. These companies ranged in size from $5 million in revenue up to $300 million. They represented the typical mid-market companies in manufacturing, distribution, and retail. I even worked with a law firm that had gotten into financial difficulties by advancing monthly partnership draws ahead of collecting their fees. Their draws were based on what they hoped to receive not what they actually received. This difference was financed by the bank until it grew to a point that the bank was unwilling to continue participating.

As it happened, none of the thirty-four companies that I worked with ended up in bankruptcy and only one ended up being sold to a competitor. One hundred percent of the loans that the banks had written off as being doubtful were recovered. Over $50 million in total loans were repaid. One company I worked with in 1975, when it was on the brink of bankruptcy, was sold for $400 million in 2021. I systematically applied the turnaround steps that I share in this book, and it was exciting to see the rapid transformation from a company where the coffin had been chosen to one that grew and prospered for many years until it was eventually sold.

Initially I was thrown in the deep end and had to quickly develop an effective turnaround process for each organization.

But as I kept working with companies of different sizes, in a broad array of industries, I started to recognize a pattern in key elements that every company exhibited. Identifying, organizing, and simplifying each stage of the process allowed me to put together quick and effective turnaround plans that applied to a range of companies and industries. Speed was a necessity and became the mother of invention.

Following the same or similar process during all the turnarounds gave me the confidence to apply it in many different types of businesses. These included retail chains, large wholesale distributors, and complex aerospace component manufacturers. Even that large law firm was turned around using the same set of principles. No matter the company size or industry, I observed very similar and frequently predictable problems. I also recognized that the same solutions would work.

Helping to turn around dozens of companies has been the greatest joy of my career. One of my hobbies is the restoration of old British cars that had been neglected over the years. The vision of what something could be, and eventually seeing it in pristine condition, is a catalyst and a great personal motivator to complete the renovation. It is also what helped me to persist when working to restore companies that appeared to be in total despair. When everyone is aligned around a shared vision, company turnarounds become genuinely enjoyable, and life-changing, for all those who participate in the renovation.

I'm writing this book today, after a nearly twenty-five-year hiatus from my turnaround work, because something extraordinary happened recently. I was asked by a group of shareholders to help turn around their company in eastern Washington. The company was a sheet metal fabricator with identical equipment to that in the company in Scotland that I'd bought. I was happy to dust off my process and incorporate methods that had worked so well in previous turnarounds in order to see what might work for this faltering company. In doing so, I found that the same challenges I had encountered decades earlier applied today. This made me realize that I'd effectively created founding principles for company turnarounds. I believed that if I could document them, they could help other people who are striving to save a company in trouble. And as you'll see in the pages that follow, these principles apply to more than company owners hoping to revive their business. They also apply to anyone who has recently bought a company and, upon opening the books, discovers that the financials are not what the seller made them out to be. In addition, I've found these principles to be immensely helpful to business owners who are getting ready to sell their company and would like to tidy up operations before selling so they can put their best foot forward. Those are just two examples. You'll see that these principles are universally applicable across a range of company sizes, industries, and circumstances, and they all work to help restore an organization's spirit, joy in their work, and vision for the future. To that end, and as a third example, one of my early readers suggested that the principles in the book would be great for an annual company retreat. It would be an effective way to see where you are as a business and to implement an overall renaissance process.

This book was also written to share with the next generation of entrepreneurs some of the insights I have gained over the last fifty years in business. My recent lectures to college students have highlighted a thirst for knowledge and unvarnished honesty. This is the first generation that has unfettered access to knowledge with tools like ChatGPT. They want to know the truth even if the emperor has no clothes.

TURNAROUNDS ARE MORE ART THAN BUSINESS

People are often surprised to learn that companies today have the same set of issues as companies that I worked with thirty or forty years ago. So many crucial elements have evolved since then: technology, business practices, work environments. I've found, however, that the process that I developed stands the test of time because human nature has not changed, and causes of business failure are human issues. That's where the art of a turnaround comes in.

Leaders of companies in severe financial distress suffer from the very human traits that prevent people from facing up to reality. Many times, their problems are so overwhelming that they feel like they are stuck in a proverbial box canyon. This is a flying term that illustrates what happens when you fly into a canyon and the canyon gets narrower and narrower and the canyon walls get steeper and steeper until you reach a point where you do not have the ability to turn around or the power to climb out.

This sense of despair is so debilitating that leaders of a dying business often go on an emotional journey that mirrors exactly what the Swiss-American psychiatrist Elisabeth Kübler-Ross came up with in her five stages of dying:

- Denial
- Anger
- Bargaining
- Depression
- Acceptance

I usually enter the turnaround process during the denial and anger stages. By simply knowing these emotions are at the forefront of a failing business, it helps us understand company leaders' sometimes irrational behavior. They get stuck looking for the third way.

Simply put, they don't like the current situation and they don't like what they will have to do to correct it because it's too painful and will reflect negatively on the leader who got them into the mess in the first place. The easiest path is to kick the can down the road until there is no more road left.

The first task for anyone attempting to lead a company turnaround is to drag the leader out of this mental slump. This applies whether you are the incumbent leader or an outsider brought in to implement the changes. The main purpose of your intervention is to create leadership where you describe the future with such confidence and optimism that all participants will willingly take that journey with you. There will be many people eloquently explaining that the vision you have is not possible or even that it was tried before and didn't work. Your leadership must display 100% confidence in your vision to overcome the doubting Thomases.

Imagine you're at the bottom of a mountain with a team of people. You need to be able to describe what the view is from the top of the mountain with such clarity and in such detail that people want to climb the mountain with you. When that happens, the true joy of a turnaround begins. You'll watch people turn from denial and anger to hope and begin to believe in a vision for the future that everyone is excited about.

THE JOY OF FINDING HIDDEN GEMS

I don't have a traditional educational background. But I was lucky enough to have the freedom to learn anything I wanted to learn when I started my own company at the age of twenty-seven. I enjoyed complexity, and solving a company's financial problems is a very complex problem with many moving parts. As mentioned, it is frequently perceived as a box canyon. With a different set of eyes and the ability to find hidden potential in many employees, I was able to find the additional power to climb out of the canyon. Much of my motivation and enjoyment came from freeing up the potential of the employees in these companies.

This potential was sitting in plain sight. What seemed obvious to me was not obvious to the owners of these businesses. Why did I look at things differently and why was the reveal so enjoyable? It comes down to the restoration of spirit and optimism. For some reason I have always been optimistic. I've also been very lucky. My friends tell me that when my toast falls on the floor it always falls with the marmalade side facing up.

Many people never really learn to read the room or to create empathy with the people they are working with. This is frequently demonstrated by many politicians and senior managers around the world. A perfect example of this was when the CEOs of the major car companies in the US flew to Washington, DC, in expensive private jets to beg for government bailouts for their failing businesses.

Many steps in the turnaround process are confrontational, needing determination, confidence, and leadership to make sure they are successfully implemented. You cannot use a baseball bat or fear to beat the skeptics and doubters into submission; you must encourage and persuade. To be successful you need to incorporate judo principles to use the energy and momentum of the skeptics to get them to go in the direction you want them to go in. Early wins provide momentum, and each win builds excitement and further momentum. You are the leader of a renaissance movement, not a funeral director; you must look and act the part. The successful accomplishment of a turnaround will be the most enjoyable work and life experiences you have ever had.

Like the renovation of a fine piece of furniture or a classic car, the work is hard and initial progress is slow but when you see the finish line it is easy to pick up the pace and complete the mission. Kind of like writing a book. This is even more rewarding when you have created a team that shares your goals of rehabilitating the company and shares the rewards.

In writing the book I found myself gravitating towards three recurring basic principles. The most interesting of these was the subject of mentoring and being mentored. From being mentored very early on in my career, it was easy to transition into being the mentor. One of the things I learned in becoming a mentor to others was that you can't want for people something they don't want for themselves. For many years I felt if only I could do a better job of motivating, if only I could be more persuasive, then they would be as excited about their future as I was. One of the early litmus tests of creating a new team in a turnaround situation was to determine what the team wanted and not what I wanted. Again, this is where the art comes in.

Over the years I tried to develop additional ways to motivate and have learned to accept less than 100% enthusiasm for everything that we were trying to accomplish during the turnaround. I also learned that instant enthusiasm frequently did not last; many of the most successful managers I worked with came from Missouri, the "Show-Me State." They were assessing me as I was assessing them. Over the years I worked with some incredible teams, all were different and responded in different ways. The cliché that "it takes all sorts" is very true in turnarounds. Looking back, I am still amazed at all the hidden gems that I found, people who flourished given the right opportunity, environment, and encouragement. The steps outlined in this book are important, but they need to be mixed with the knowledge that you cannot do it on your own. The art is reading the room and acting quickly and effectively regardless of the challenges that you face.

The ten steps outlined in this book are straightforward and have been battle-tested on the front lines during my own turnarounds. They will hopefully give you direction and confidence to revive a company that is in financial trouble. For me it has been a wonderfully fulfilling journey that has led to the full restoration of the companies I worked with. The vision of a successful company with happy, motivated employees working in harmony replacing the despair associated with financial failure has always provided me with energy and motivation to do the hard work. Unless the bailiffs are actually at the door, it is never too late to start the restoration process. This book shows you a place to start and places to focus on when everything around you in the company appears to be crashing down. I recommend that the steps be followed sequentially but some can be done concurrently. All the steps include both art and process.

LEADERSHIP, MOMENTUM, CONFIDENCE, purpose, and vision are all art forms and are more effective when used together with a defined process. I have tried to show how important the art is, as well as the process and the joy that can be achieved in the restoration of a company. There is a wonderful British television show called *The Repair Shop* where guests bring in treasured items that have seen better times. The guests leave the items with this incredibly eclectic group of artisans whose step-by-step processes restore them to their previous glory. The guests then return. At the reveal, it is heartwarming to see the joy of the guests when they see their fully restored treasure and the joy of the team that engineered the transformation. It is this joy that I hope you can experience yourself when you successfully accomplish your first turnaround.

THE THREE PILLARS BEHIND EVERY SUCCESSFUL TURNAROUND

The philosophy behind my turnaround process sits upon three distinct pillars that intersect to create a natural form of optimism. These ingredients to a holistic approach to turnarounds prioritize a shared vision for the future, joy, and tapping into people's strengths. This will transport everyone to an exciting destination.

The three pillars are **mentorship, the elimination of constraints**, and **the pursuit of happiness**. They have formed not only my business philosophy but also a life philosophy that has allowed me the privilege of reinvigorating companies and their employees and helping them create an exciting vision for the future that was eminently achievable. I truly believe that taking the time to understand and prioritize these pillars can be life-changing for anyone.

The best way to understand how the pillars drive my turn-around work is to also learn a bit about the role they've played in my personal and professional life. As I write this, I am seventy-six years old and can say that I have had a profoundly happy, exciting, enjoyable, and eventful life. I've achieved financial success beyond my wildest dreams; I live in a country I feel blessed to call home; and I revel in the joy that my family brings me every day. This may sound smug and conceited, but I assure you that it comes from a place of profound gratitude, wonder, and awe at what I've been able to achieve by having the determination to follow my own path.

My career started in earnest when I emigrated to the United States from England on September 25, 1973. Prior to that I had had the good fortune to enter the computer business in 1967 when one of my first mentors, Charlie Ross, hired me at eighteen years old. I'd answered an ad in the national *Daily Telegraph* newspaper announcing an open exam for a job that would involve working with the most advanced computers at the time. Anyone could apply; there were no prerequisite qualifications. Applicants were tested with an examination based entirely on their ability to solve logic problems. I didn't know exactly what the job would entail but was excited about the idea that they were looking for outliers and people who had the ability to solve problems that were not obvious. Four weeks after the exam, I received a formal letter saying I was one of eight people hired out of eight hundred who had applied.

I eagerly accepted the job, having no idea how it was going to change my life forever.

MENTORSHIP

Charlie Ross was the embodiment of mentorship. He was a wonderfully flamboyant dreamer who gave me opportunities that even now still fill me with awe. Maybe he saw a kindred spirit in me; I will never know. What I saw in Charlie was an indomitable spirit that would vanquish anyone who got in his way.

On our first day at the job, Charlie informed us that he was going to help us become the most technically advanced computing team in the UK. He'd provide us with two professors from Imperial College London, one of the most advanced universities for the study of computer sciences. For the next two years, we were to learn everything there was to know about computers: mathematics, coding, advanced Boolean algebra—all of it.

Charlie stuck to his word. For two years, we were trained by the professors who pounded into each of our brains the value of simplicity in computing and problem-solving (Occam's razor). I was encouraged to think creatively and to start every project from a blank slate. Realizing that I had a knack for solving complex problems provided me with a new level of confidence. For the first time in my life, I grasped that I could confidently build things in my mind and convert them to a language that would run the computer. Competence bred confidence.

Shortly after our training was completed, Charlie Ross summoned me into his office with a new idea. His company had recently purchased two Sperry UNIVAC 418 computers. He believed the computers had significantly more capability than the people who designed them envisioned. Charlie believed it would be possible to connect the Sperry UNIVAC computers to terminals all over London using teletype printers and local phone lines. This idea was a step change in how computers could be used. He'd been working with a group of stockbrokers in The City (London's financial center) and was looking for a way to speed up their communication.

His idea was to set up terminals in the stockbrokers' office so they could enter real-time information about their customers and store it in one of the storage drums. On the other storage drum, he planned to store all the clients' stock holdings. By reading the paper tape of all transactions from the London Stock Exchange each day, he could offer close-of-business pricing. With this information, the entire portfolio of the holdings of a major bank could be calculated and printed out in minutes. This process used to take up to three weeks by hand, and during that time the values of their stocks could have changed significantly.

This was 1967 and nothing like this had never been tried before. Charlie was a true trailblazer. No one had ever created an end-of-day pricing for the stock market. Stockbrokers at this time were not using computers to store their customer information. The idea they could now store information safely and securely on a remote computer was a giant act of faith.

Charlie also told me about another device that he had found in America, called a Harris Photon typesetter. This device would be a game changer in the printing business. My job was to create an interface between this device and the main Sperry UNIVAC computer. He believed we could use it to create a printed book of the stock market results overnight. Before Charlie's idea, the process was done by hand and took up to five weeks. By that time the market could have changed drastically and the information would be out of date.

Charlie tasked me with leading the team that would bring his vision to life. I was stunned and thrilled by the challenge. Charlie gave twenty-year-old me enormous responsibility to solve complex problems that were at the leading edge of computer science at the time. Although we had no idea then, we realized later on that we had developed the world's first software as a service (SaaS) company in 1967 called SCAN (Stock Market Computer Answering Network), a precursor to today's Bloomberg financial system.

Charlie's vision and mentorship changed my life. It wasn't just the technical training I received under his leadership, but the immense confidence he instilled in me by believing I could solve such complex problems. He showed me how to unlock the doors that prevent so many people from achieving their potential.

I owe similar gratitude to so many other mentors who have shaped my life. When I was in boarding school, a wonderful professor, Dr. Martyn Cundy, went out of his way to challenge and encourage me when my other teachers only saw an irresponsible fourteen-year-old. He spotted my unusual knack for mathematics when he noticed I always received perfect grades on my exams despite having never completed any of my assignments. Rather than scold me for my incomplete work, he encouraged me by taking me out of my classroom of fourteen-year-olds and letting me take the math class for eighteen-year-olds. He gave me extraordinary confidence that I had capabilities that were different, and encouraged me to embrace them.

Jumping ahead to my early days in Seattle, Dave Friedenberg, the banker in charge of the jewelry company's loan, gave me my first major turnaround opportunity in 1974. He also gave his unwavering support and confidence in my ability to turn around companies—a job for which I had no formal training or qualifications. This is what mentors do: they nurture our strengths, and their guidance lives on long after they're gone.

I mentioned that the opportunity to unlock human potential is one of the great joys in turnaround work. Mentorship plays such a key role in that process. As I get to know each person in a company, I prioritize listening to their story and look for their strengths. The process takes time. Mentorship can only happen once trust is earned, so your first step is to enter a turnaround situation as a confident leader with a clear vision that will help the company. As you work with everyone to bring that vision to life, trust and relationships build. People's talents and passions come to the foreground. As a leader, your role is to help each member of your team flourish, and mentorship finds its place within that environment of growth and support.

ELIMINATING CONSTRAINTS

The three pillars overlap and intersect throughout the course of a turnaround. Eliminating constraints has strong ties to mentorship. I've come to realize that most constraints holding us back are artificial, and a significant part of creating the new momentum in a turnaround is to remove these constraints. They come in many varieties: *I'm not qualified and therefore I cannot do that job; we do not have the money and therefore we cannot implement what you are recommending;* and so on.

Constraints need to be systematically removed. This does two things: (1) it shows that they are artificial, and (2) it shows how easily they can be removed. This creates an entirely different mindset for everybody going forward.

The cornerstone of each turnaround I've completed was the moment artificial constraints were eliminated. Artificial constraints stop individuals from making decisions that can change their own direction in life and the direction of a company. Many are self-imposed and block genuine creative solutions from ever being tried. Removing these constraints creates a whole new attitude of what is possible.

If we want to see what's possible when artificial constraints are eliminated, look at Elon Musk and SpaceX. When he decided to get into the space business, he went down to NASA and asked them why satellite launching was so expensive. They explained it's because rockets go up and then are thrown away. When he asked why they couldn't bring the rockets back, the folks at NASA laughed at him. That was an absolute constraint for them, but Musk was determined to try. NASA thought he was mad (they may have been right). When the first rockets blew up trying to land, NASA's attitude was "I told you so." When he succeeded, it was just crickets. Of course, SpaceX's work is immensely complex, but their approach to achieve what others thought was impossible is simple: they eliminated artificial constraints that others saw as absolutes.

Personally, the elimination of constraints allowed me to change my life forever when I made the decision to emigrate to the US on September 25, 1973. I could now take my six years' computer experience and start a journey in a country where I believed the opportunities were limitless horizons with no constraints, artificial or otherwise.

The American Dream is sometimes dismissed by those who have not had the opportunity to take advantage of it, so I consider myself one of the lucky ones. I arrived with

$300 and no formal qualifications, but I had the advantage of seeing the potential in the US and the prospects of a nascent computer industry.

One of my favorite parts of turnaround work is showing people, and companies, how much they're capable of when they remove artificial constraints. And there are many ways to do this, particularly in situations where a person's job can be expanded or silos can be torn down. So often, employees are constrained from doing something because it doesn't fall within their job description. They weren't given permission to do it, so they stayed in their silo. Once you start opening up the scope of what people can do, you unlock a new level of confidence. This is often how we discover wonderful gems within a company—once people's limitations are removed, they blossom and begin working to their full potential.

PURSUIT OF HAPPINESS

Notice that it's not *happiness*; it's the *pursuit of happiness*. This is a unique right that is found in the preamble of the Constitution of the United States and it's at the heart of the American Dream. Happiness can come in many forms, not just the accumulation of wealth. In fact, pursuing happiness in the broadest possible terms includes creating an environment of happiness for others.

A powerful part of my turnaround work is when I ask people what would make them happy at their job. This usually shocks them for two reasons: (1) they'd never had an employer ask them such a thing, even in the best of times, and (2) when a company is in financial distress, pursuing happiness is the last thing on anybody's mind. People are depressed. They have no vision for the future. There is no happiness in a company that is having financial problem. Suppliers are not shipping. The owner looks terrified. Everybody's wondering when the next shoe is going to drop. However, simply asking employees what one thing they would change to make their job more enjoyable can have a profound effect. Sometimes eliminating those things that make a person unhappy is the answer, or at least part of the answer, so they and the company can start moving in a positive direction.

The pursuit of happiness is a process, and the major part of that process is eliminating what makes you unhappy. If every day you come to work and there is an item or a part of your job that makes you miserable, then this does not auger well for pursuing happiness. It is up to the leader of a company to seek out and eliminate elements that make jobs disagreeable, boring, and unfulfilling.

I can't deny that there will be some unhappy people in a turnaround situation. It's likely that some employees won't be selected to stay with the company, but leaders have a tremendous responsibility to let people go with empathy. There is no easy way of telling someone that they no longer have a job. But if you avoid that hard part of the work, you're jeopardizing the entire company and eventually everyone will lose their job. You have to triage. You have to decide who you can keep, how much you can pay, and what structure you need to survive. For the team members you do keep, putting them on a path of pursuing happiness at work will benefit them all, and the company.

MORE COMPANIES NEED TURNAROUNDS THAN WE TEND TO THINK

Turnarounds are not just for failing companies. The principles here were developed for organizations on the brink of collapse, but nearly any company would benefit from the revival that these ten steps bring about. This method gets a company back to basics by uncovering the destructive elements and getting rid of them. Those things can be people and processes. After going through the process outlined in this book what is left is a sustainable enjoyable company with a fully aligned team working around a shared vision. You don't have to be failing financially to enjoy a complete company refresh.

WHEN A CIRCUMSTANCE WARRANTS A TURNAROUND

I've seen the turnaround process be incredibly restorative for businesses even when there isn't the need for immediate action in a financial turnaround scenario. The following are four examples of this situation.

Recently Acquired Companies

The process of buying a company is fraught with difficulties. The buyer wishes to pay as little as possible and the seller wishes to get the maximum amount they can. The difficulty is getting both parties to agree. The seller puts a value over and above the book value based on the amount of effort they feel they have expended over many years building the company. The buyer, on the other hand, is looking at the company strictly in financial terms and the ability to get a return on their investment. This conundrum ends with the buyer almost always paying too much for the company. As I have seen with many acquisitions I have been involved in, the process is long and torturous, requiring both skill in due diligence and determination to complete the task.

After working on an acquisition for many months, there is a great desire on the buyer's side to complete the transaction. The invitations to the wedding have been sent out, the reception hall has been booked, and it's too difficult emotionally to back out. This is where the buyer will make considerable concessions to close the deal. This process inevitably leads to buyer's remorse. On Day 1, they are faced with a company that is way less profitable than they thought and a company that they have paid too much for. Although the buyer had not planned a turnaround, a turnaround is now urgently needed. The dog chased the car and finally caught it. Now what?

It is estimated that in 2022, close to 100,000 businesses were sold in North America. All these companies experienced a Day 1 under new ownership. As the new sheriff in town, implementing a company turnaround is now an effective way to dramatically improve the prospects of a new acquisition and produce the planned return on investment (ROI).

Business Owners Preparing to Sell Their Company

Smart homeowners refresh and stage their property so it shows in the best possible light when it is put on the market. Business owners would be wise to do the same. This not only maximizes your sale price but also takes a great deal of pain out of the selling process. Imagine presenting potential buyers with a company that's lean, efficient, and thriving financially. No smoke-and-mirrors accounting practices are necessary because there would be nothing to hide. This sort of clean slate would give a seller significant negotiating power.

Companies with New Leadership

The turnaround process can be a lifeline for new business owners tasked with cleaning up old business practices. Sometimes that new leadership is family. It's a tale as old as time. A retiring business owner passes the family business down to a child, or children, and the recipient is excited to lead the company into the next era. Only once the excitement has subsided and the financials have been given a proper look, dread and panic sink in. Mom and Dad hadn't been running the company as efficiently as everyone had thought. In fact, it may be a wonder that payroll had even been met in recent years.

Whether a new leader is left to clean up their parents' mess, or they've stepped into a floundering company as a new hire, a company refresh is an essential first step.

Companies that Have Lost Their Way

This is sometimes the plight of start-ups that grew very quickly. What began as a single founder or a couple of friends with a dream morphs into head-spinning rounds of funding, hiring, and scaling. The end result barely resembles the original vision. Often, founders stop to look around and realize they need a renaissance. They want to revive certain founding principles and discard unnecessary practices that have crept into their company. A turnaround helps to restart the energy and get a company back to their roots.

Even for established companies, that kind of self-check can be very valuable. The turnaround process can be used as an annual retreat exercise. Walking through the 10 Steps each year will help make sure they haven't fallen back into old habits, or developed new ones that don't mesh with the company's vision.

WHEREVER YOU FIND yourself when you pick up this book, know that it's designed not only for business owners and senior executives. It's also for new leaders that have been brought into a company with a mission to make significant improvements quickly without the slash and burn of the tradition management consultants. The 10 Step process creates a road map for the renovation of a company—for anyone taking on the task, and for whatever reason that company may find itself in need of a reset.

It's also important to realize, however, that not every company is worth turning around. There needs to be some sign of life left to make the effort worthwhile. Sometimes the financials are truly irreparable, or the company is entrenched in a dying industry that has no future. Most companies are worth saving, but before you forge ahead, make sure there's still a heartbeat under the rubble to warrant your efforts at revival.

You also need to be a leader with a vision and have people who are willing to pursue that vision with you. You may not know who those people are just yet. But it's important to have a sense that they're there, somewhere in the organization. One of the first steps in the process is finding them. From there, you'll be well on your way to a new beginning.

WHEN THE UNEXPECTED FORCES A TURNAROUND

Sometimes turnarounds are necessary when we least expect them. That's what I discovered with my aerospace manufacturing company back in 2001. We went from a rapidly growing company to one that had its projected sales reduced by 30% in one day.

One of the companies I helped restore in my early days working with Dave Friedenberg and his bank turned out to be especially intriguing to me. They supplied Boeing Company with precision components that were installed on all models of their airplanes. The complexity of the manufacturing process and the requirements for perfect quality were extremely challenging but also very rewarding intellectually. I had finally found an industry for which I had a real passion.

It was at this point I negotiated a more attractive financial arrangement for my turnaround work, an equity position that I could liquidate when the company achieved profitability. I repeated this process with two other manufacturing companies. After I had liquidated my equity positions, I had the resources to acquire my own small aerospace component manufacturing company. Utilizing all the invaluable experience I had acquired during my turnarounds, I grew the company from $1 million in revenue to $30 million in a ten-year period. Black swan events can impact even well-run companies, so when 9/11 occurred, the sales in the company dropped more than 30%. The latter part of 2001 was a devastating time in the aerospace industry, and it did not fully recover for the next four years.

The following chapters include discussion about contingency plans and how the turnaround process can effectively be used to create them. I had such a contingency plan at the ready in the top right-hand drawer of my desk. One week after 9/11, we started to implement a very aggressive reduction in force with decisions already made as to who would be retained. We were one of the few profitable aerospace companies in 2002. I never thought I would be turning around my own company, but my background proved very helpful as I was faced with an extraordinary black swan event.

I also called on my computer background to develop a quality system to eliminate defects in manufacturing. I eventually called this company Net-Inspect. At the time I had no idea that this was going to turn out to be another wonderfully serendipitous event. The manufacturing group had many visitors from major aerospace companies around the world, and they all expressed interest in the software. I did not want to get into the software installation business with big companies and all their bureaucracy, so I told them I was not interested in selling the software to them.

It was when I was driving down to one of my facilities in Portland, Oregon, that I had an epiphany: if I put the software on a group of secured servers, I could offer it as a service. That's precisely what I did. This was in 1998 and I believe we became one of the first software as a service companies in the world using the Internet. A strange twist given my first introduction to computers in 1967—perhaps my early experience with Charlie Ross was recovered from the deep recesses of my brain. In 2012, I sold my manufacturing group to focus on Net-Inspect. This was a wise decision given the turmoil in the aerospace industry with delays in Boeing's 787, grounding of its 737 MAX, and delay in its 777X. Talk about black swan events.

Net-Inspect has prospered and is now the most widely used quality software in the aerospace industry with over eight thousand companies using the software in fifty-six countries. I believe that Net-Inspect wouldn't be the company it is today if I hadn't had that contingency plan in my desk drawer more than two decades ago.

FOR ALL OUR DIFFERENCES, WE ARE VERY MUCH THE SAME

There are many different types of business, plus hybrids of them, but all ultimately fall into one of four categories. Although they are different in types of structure, they have more similarities than differences and therefore the turn-around principles in this book are equally applicable and effective regardless of the type of business. Each needs to manage cash flow and to have customers, suppliers, and employees. For all the seeming differences, the fundamentals are still the same. The four categories of business are:

1. Retail (including online without any bricks and mortar)
2. Services (including software development and SaaS providers)
3. Distributors
4. Manufacturers

I spend a bit more time on manufacturing companies due to their complexity and the difficulty of unraveling their financial status quickly. In a manufacturing company there are many moving parts, but you'll see how even the most complex companies can be quickly deconstructed, rebuilt, and returned to profitability.

WE'RE ABOUT TO NEED TURNAROUNDS MORE THAN EVER

The next few years are going to be very disruptive. Our pre- and post-COVID easy money, low- or no-cost borrowing, and close-to-zero interest rates have been exacerbated by unprecedented federal borrowing and spending. As I write this in 2024, the inevitable has happened: interest rates are climbing at the fastest rate in modern economic history and the monetary tightening to combat inflation has just started. Many companies that were swept up in the euphoria of zero interest will be looking at some very challenging times.

The days of wine and roses are over. Companies are being confronted with a new reality and an economic climate that many in the younger generation have never seen. Many companies face bleak prospects and an immediate need to reinvent themselves. This has happened before and those of us who have been through these scenarios many times before are in a unique position to dust off the manuals that have been sitting on a shelf for the last few years. This is what I have done with this book. Remarkably, virtually everything that I had in my recovery templates is still totally applicable today. There are universal truths that are timeless and always relevant. I feel excited about sharing this information with a new generation precisely because of its universal truths. One of the most important of these is how to you should treat and respect your fellow travelers. They should be treated in a way that you would like to be treated yourself.

There is a brand-new generation that has never experienced a severe economic downturn. I hope this book prepares them and is an economic lifeboat. Even if the economic downturn is not severe, my hope is that this book helps readers improve the lives of those they work with as well as those who work for them.

THE 10 STEPS TO TURNING A COMPANY AROUND

This chapter is an aerial view. The rest of this book walks you through the 10 Steps for turning a company around, with details and examples of what each looks like in practice. The sum of these parts will be a company revival that far exceeds what anyone may have thought possible.

STEP 1: ESTABLISHING LEADERSHIP

Establishing leadership starts with an honest meeting with the existing leadership team. This meeting will give you a good indication of the current team's willingness to work with you and implement the difficult changes that are required in a turnaround. It is also your first step in building trust as the leader of this company renaissance. At this stage no personnel decisions are made about who will make up the leadership team going forward, but it is a great time to start mentally putting the building blocks in place. In the first meeting, it's important to observe who has enthusiasm and energy for change, and who hasn't. The company Jeremiahs always self-identify. Honesty is not a bad thing in identifying how serious the problems are but if individuals show an unwillingness to try new things, then they are not suited for the battle ahead. As Shakespeare wrote in *Henry V*, "he which hath no stomach to this fight, / Let him depart."

STEP 2: FINANCIAL AND CASH ASSESSMENT

Step 2 is dedicated to uncovering and simplifying the company's financial information so you can create a realistic go-forward plan. This is such an important step, and one often met with the most resistance. It's common for many people to shy away from finance and accounting. It's a subject matter full of strange words and lots of foreboding. Accountants are trained to speak a different language and answer any questions with unintelligible words or, "it depends." Getting a straight answer from a CFO or accountant is like trying to pick up a piece of soap in the shower. I do not have an accounting degree, a CPA, or any formal background in accounting. What I do have is the ability to learn and ask questions. This does require confidence, and in this early part of the turnaround process, that is an essential ingredient for success. If there is anything you do not understand, keep asking questions until you have an intelligible answer. You are not supposed to understand the numbers; these are the purview of the financial department, which will only let you know what they think you need to know. Financial structures are organized like Egyptian hieroglyphics: unintelligible by anybody outside the clan, and you have no way of confirming whether or not they are correct. Now is the time to get back to basics and probe until you fully understand.

It's not possible to put together a credible go-forward plan until the company's current financial situation is fully understood and verified. The glossary on page 221 will help you quickly decipher some of the terms and more arcane practices of accounting. By the end of this step, you will have determined a clear and precise financial plan that lays out what changes need to be made. The plan also shows which steps need to be taken immediately in order to right the ship.

STEP 3: COMPANY MEETINGS

By this stage you have a good understanding, in broad terms, of what needs to be done. In Step 3, you'll bring those ideas to the staff in small company meetings. This is your first step into the future as you start to show employees that you are there to help make their company a better place to work. A series of small company meetings are your opportunity to get everyone's input and ideas, and to assess who should be on the turnaround team. A simple starting point is to ask each employee, "What is one thing that annoys you most when you come to work?" This reveals an item that causes antagonism every day. Removing these items can have a very positive effect on overall morale.

I recommend having no more than ten people in each meeting. It is also important that no employee has their direct supervisor in the same meeting as this may inhibit their input for fear of retribution. This is a very valuable time to solicit employees' recommendations and suggestions. All need to be documented, whether or not they are immediately possible, advisable, or logical to implement; those judgment calls will come. At this point, all recommendations and suggestions should be considered and published publicly throughout the company, with an implementation date noted. This lets the employees know that their recommendations are being taken seriously.

Very quickly, the overall momentum in the company will change since publication of the employee recommendations shows that management not only is listening but also values employee input and recommendations. This process always elicits more recommendations and a greater participation of everyone in the turnaround process.

STEP 4: PERSONNEL ASSESSMENT

This is one of the most difficult steps: the day you need to create your go-forward team. Your first priority is your management and supervisory personnel. You are not only deciding the pros and cons of each individual but also basing those decisions on what the company can afford. This is also the time to do a deep dive into what individual employees actually do to determine any overlaps or consolidations that can be done.

Besides explaining the process for making the final selections, this chapter describes how to handle communication of those decisions to employees being kept on and those being cut. It is important to preserve the dignity of employees who did not make the cut. This is the time to thank the employees who are to be cut for their contribution and to let them know that, if the financial circumstances had been different, you would not have had to make such difficult decisions. It is also important to hold out a carrot: no promises but a possibility of being rehired when the company returns to profitability. The selected employees need to be told that there will be no more cuts. If greater savings are required, then everyone's pay will be reduced across the board.

STEP 5: IMPLEMENTATION OF EMPLOYEE RECOMMENDATIONS

Prior to Step 5, the new leadership needs to have put together a detailed plan on how to implement as many of the employee recommendations as possible. To kick off this stage of the turnaround, Step 5 focuses on how to plan a three-day weekend renovation for the whole facility—what I call building a barn in a day. The story of the Scottish company that I share on page 118 is a great example of doing that.

STEP 6: BUSINESS ASSESSMENT

By now you should have a good grasp of where the business is at and what needs to be done going forward. Step 6 looks at the business as a whole and consider factors like: Who is the competition? Who are the customers? Where does your company fit into the competitive landscape? What additional changes need to be made to give the company the best prospects going forward? You'll continue to build out your plan based on where the company stands on each of these items.

STEP 7: STAKEHOLDER MEETINGS

This is the first time you'll share your turnaround plan with parties outside the company. The key stakeholders to meet with are your bank, investors, suppliers, and customers. Once the business assessment is complete, addressing each of these groups honestly is a critical step. This is not a time to sugarcoat any issues; it is a time to under-promise and over-deliver. Remember the life insurance salesman's motto, "If at first you don't succeed, that's it!" You have only one chance to create confidence in the future so make the most of it: hide nothing.

Honesty is always the best policy even if it means telling a supplier that you cannot pay for their goods at the previously agreed-upon price or a customer that you are unable to sell products to them at the current price. Remember what the football coach said to one of his players who approached him for a pay raise after a losing season: "We lost with you, and we can lose without you." Confronting a customer or supplier with the news that they are the proximate cause of the company's problems requires finesse, but you will be surprised at how often they already know you cannot stay viable with their pricing. They will try to get away with it for as long as possible but will not be surprised when you finally turn up at their door.

STEP 8: QUALITY AND PROCESS IMPROVEMENT

Quality and process improvement can be one of the largest areas of cost savings. It can also be a good way to differentiate yourself from your competition. If you are manufacturing a product and make it correctly every time, your costs will be way lower than your competition that has to deal with rework, warranty claims, and returns. In Step 8, you are looking for the real root causes of quality issues: this is key to resolving them. In addition, having defined, robust processes and following them is critical to maintaining a high level of quality for the future. Poor quality can do immense damage to a brand, as many companies have realized too late, after the quality issues are made public.

A big part of improving your processes will involve automating as much as you can. So much is possible with the advent of new technologies that can transform companies. Tasks that used to be manual and paper-driven and that required a high level of expertise are now replaced with cloud technology, natural language processing, and machine learning. Belief in technology sends the message that the leader of the company believes in the future.

Optimizing your processes will also eliminate the need for your departments of corrections. Companies often have staff dedicated to correcting what other employees failed to do correctly. By making sure everything is done correctly at the right quality level in the first place, you eliminate the need to redo work. Eliminating defects in all aspects of your business will streamline your organization without any reduction in productivity and with a significant increase in profitability.

STEP 9: INVENTORY AND EQUIPMENT VALUATION AND ASSESSMENT

This chapter walks you through the detailed process of valuing your inventory and equipment (the glossary on page 221 includes a detailed description of how inventory is valued). The most important aspect of Step 9 is the actual count of the inventory, at what is called the lower of cost or market value. You may have a higher than market value on your books; this needs to be adjusted to reflect actual market value. The same applies to equipment. This is one place where what is on the books may understate the actual value because of depreciation. Well-maintained equipment retains a lot of its value, while poorly maintained equipment does not. Equipment that has had jerry-rigged repairs not only may have a significant value impairment but also can be a liability if someone gets hurt using it.

Step 9 also shines a light on the value of equipment replacement. There is nothing that sends a more positive message to employees than new equipment. It indicates and restores confidence in the future and confidence in employees.

STEP 10: COMPANY PRESENTATION OF THE GO-FORWARD PLAN

Step 10 is presentation of the full plan to the entire team. This includes expectations and complete confidence that the plan will not only work but also be exceeded. This is the time to outline which job you are going to take on personally. Hold monthly meetings to highlight the wins and discuss how items that have still not been achieved are going to be achieved.

Communicate all changes and try to make them visible. After building the barn in a day, many of the changes will be visible; however, that becomes the new norm. Photograph and document the way it was and how it looks today to remind everyone of what was achieved. This will give everyone a sense of pride and accomplishment.

ONCE YOU BEGIN the turnaround, there must be no way back (see Conclusion: Burn the Ships à la Cortés). Any backsliding must be stopped in its tracks. After all the work that everyone in the company has put in, it would be a tragedy to waste it. Remember that any process improvement is elastic and the tendency is for it to go back to its original state. Close off the exit ramps and stay on the freeway to prosperity.

STEP 1

ESTABLISHING LEADERSHIP

Your first day is critical. This is the day that the company's momentum and direction change, and a new vision is formed. It's also the day that you begin to establish trust as the leader of the turnaround.

The first task on Day 1 is to get together the management team, all department heads, and all supervisors. This is the first group to whom you'll present the new vision. This may not be the team going forward as there may be subtractions and additions from among direct-line employees. At some time in the future, you can add people, but the focus initially is to work with the current team.

Establishing momentum and differentiating from the past is harder for the existing chief executive officer (CEO), but it can be achieved very effectively. There is an obvious human element that has to be taken into account: fear.

Change is always frightening for the incumbents and the leader needs to establish that tough and difficult decisions are not only going to be made but also going to be made quickly and effectively.

Your approach requires a delicate balance of empathy and efficiency. For example, at this meeting you'll need to address that some jobs will inevitably be eliminated. An analogy that I have always used to explain this situation is that of an NFL team: it starts with ninety football players at the beginning of training season and must reduce its roster to a maximum of fifty-three players by the time the season starts. The thirty-seven players let go are all world-class players, but unfortunately there is a limit to the number of players a team can keep. This scenario parallels when it is established that a company can only afford to keep a certain number of employees to stay in business. This does not mean that those not selected were in any way less competent; it is simply that the financial rules of survival require that reductions be made.

This analogy tends to resonate. Although it does not mitigate the impact of people losing their jobs, it hopefully allows them to retain some pride knowing their departure was caused not by their own actions but by circumstances beyond their control. This is one of the reasons why reducing the team needs to be done quickly, compassionately, and only once. It is important to convey the message that this is one and done and the team that remains will see the complete turn-around through. If more cost reductions are necessary, they will come from across-the-board reductions of everyone's pay with a higher percentage reduction at the top-management level. This communication is very important and genuinely sets the stage for healthy recovery.

Step 1 sets the energy and momentum for the entire turnaround. Having started with a meeting of all company leaders, you then move on to two meetings that will be especially eye-opening: one with the company chief financial officer (CFO) and one with the person who has been with the company the longest. Throughout the process, you'll set the tone that a new day has come, and that the company is on a path to prosperity with you as their leader.

FIRST ORDER OF BUSINESS: MAKE IT CLEAR THERE'S A NEW SHERIFF IN TOWN

The moment you walk in the door, it has to be obvious that someone new is taking charge. One way to do this is through very demonstrative changes. Things have to look different. Whenever I lead a company turnaround, one of the first changes I make is to take over the current chief executive's office, remove their desk, and put a conference table in its place. If it's your office, do the same. This small but powerful change is a symbol of the collaborative environment you're creating.

I also remove all named parking spots so that parking is first come, first served. If you want the best spot, come in first. This flattens the hierarchy, which is a critical part of the turnaround process. Again, you're creating a new, democratized environment where all ideas are listened to and considered. A simple change like removing assigned parking spots sends a signal that everybody matters equally. As the leader, practice being first in but do not take the best spot. In fact, take the worst spot to show a little humility.

It is a new day and you are going to forge a new direction. If you're the incumbent leader, you personally have to look and act differently. People won't have confidence in the leader who led them into the box canyon, but if you start taking actions that you should have taken prior to getting the company into trouble, you can reclaim trust.

Start at the initial meeting by admitting that the current state of the company is entirely your fault as the leader/CEO. Don't blame others, your employees, your suppliers, your customers, the weather, the economy, COVID, or climate change. The reason the company is having problems is because you as a leader failed to respond to any or all of the previous indications of problems. You have now recognized what you have done wrong and you are taking steps to correct the problems. Also make it clear that you want input and suggestions since you do not have all the answers.

Even if you are the old sheriff, you need to act and look like the new sheriff in town. Habits like holing up in your office, looking depressed, and blaming others are a thing of the past. Now everything is positive and you have a definitive plan that will improve everyone's lives and make working for your company more enjoyable. Confidence breeds confidence so it's important not to be threatening even though you will be making difficult and painful decisions. The time for easy decisions is long gone and part of creating a new confidence is honesty. You need to communicate that you'll be making some very difficult decisions, but without coming across in an intimidating way. This is a fine balance. There needs to be some fear in order to motivate change; however, it cannot be used as a baseball bat or you will have little or no cooperation. It's helpful to put yourself in the position of the recipients to determine the best way to convey both the difficulties and the opportunities that the company is facing.

If you are not the incumbent and have been brought in to help the company, or you have recently acquired the company or inherited it, then dwelling on the past does no good. Focusing on the future is all that counts. Almost invariably, if the company has recently been purchased, the buyer will have paid too much. Sometimes this is caused by poor due diligence; sometimes it can be caused by gross misrepresentation. It is what it is, and like golf, we need to hit the ball where it lies not where we would like it to be. There are outside remedies for blatant fraud and for representations and warranties that the seller may have made that turned out to be completely false. This is not the time to dwell on those because if recovery is not possible you still own the company. An effective turnaround can make a poor purchase decision into a good overall decision to acquire a company.

Smile with confidence ("it takes a worried man to sing a worried song"). Confidence is contagious and making decisions reinforces that a new day has arrived. You as the leader are the new metronome; now is the time to dramatically pick up the pace. Meetings need to be stand-ups and short; decisions need to be made quickly and with conviction; and everything needs to keep moving.

Another immediate action to indicate that you as the leader have changed is to make sure that on Day 1 you arrive first and leave last. Be upbeat and indicate to everyone that you are going to put together a plan and execute it as quickly as possible, and that the results are going to be dramatic, visible, and effective.

Describing the future as you envision it is a great way to eliminate a lot of people's natural fears. This is a gradual process and needs concrete deliverables early on in your tenure to convince the skeptics that what you have envisioned is going to take place. To start, describe a future where the factory is cleaned and has new equipment, people get pay raises, and the company is more competitive. You can keep the details broad for now. The point is to describe what you genuinely think the company can be, and to convey with certainty that this turnaround is the route that will get the company there. This is likely the first piece of good news most employees will have heard at work in years.

If you are not the incumbent, it's important to make sure people do not feel threatened. Obviously, there will be some natural apprehension of a new person in charge. The way to overcome this is to be personable. Talk with as many people as possible. Acknowledge that there will be many changes, but that they will make the company a better place to work and the work more enjoyable. You want to be fair but firm. There will still be apprehension but very quickly people will start to trust you as long as you're honest and forthright about the problems and the steps that are going to be needed to turn the company around.

CREATE A SAFE HARBOR FOR EMPLOYEES TO BE HONEST

You can't bring real change to a company unless you truly understand the problems that need to be fixed. The financials will tell you a lot, but you also need your people to be honest with you about what's going on. Establishing yourself as a trustworthy leader is essential for this. People need to feel comfortable that you would be receptive to everybody's input, and not just listen to the senior managers who had effectively gotten the company in trouble in the first place. But those senior managers need to feel safe, too. If they're at the top of a company that's in such dire trouble, they're likely holding on to some troubling secrets that you need to know about.

A simple way to encourage people to open up is by taking time during that first meeting to assure them that the consequences of telling the truth won't be fatal to them. This organically creates a sort of confessional where they're comfortable being honest. People likely won't jump to tell you everything at that first meeting, but creating that listening platform lets them know your door is open. I've also found that if I can anticipate a problem and bring it to light myself, it creates instant relief for the person who had been hiding it. For instance, if I tell the CFO that I think the inventory is overstated by $2 million and that we need to write off that $2 million, he'll likely think, *At last, someone finally knows the truth*. When you relieve them of that burden and invite them to come clean with a promise of zero consequences, you can get to the heart of the problems you need to address.

On the flip side, sometimes you need to be a little ruthless to get to the truth. This can be especially true if you've been brought in as an outsider and tasked with uncovering foul play. If you find yourself in this position, it is a good idea to come in a day earlier than expected. This allows you to see things as they normally are rather than altered prior to your arrival.

Many years ago, I was asked by the board of directors of a Belgian company to visit their US plant in South Carolina to find out what was going on. The board was suspicious that all was not what it seemed, but they were unable to see what the problems were because they were so well hidden. Luckily, they were hidden in plain sight. I arrived a day early to their plant, much to the consternation of the CEO. The executive parking lot was filled with virtually brand-new Cadillacs purchased as company cars. All previous visits from the Belgian board had been announced in advance, which allowed the executives to bring in their wives' more modest cars on meeting days and hide their Cadillacs from the prying eyes of the board of directors.

As someone who has been brought in, or even as an insider, you need to do the unexpected. This allows you to control the narrative and make sure everything is exposed for scrutiny.

OBSERVE WHO IS WITH YOU AND WHO IS NOT

That first meeting with company leaders can be very revealing. Observing how the participants react will give you a good indication of whether or not they wish to be part of the long-term solution. It's important to determine who wants to work with you and who will be working against you. The quicker you establish who your main management team should be, the quicker you can move to the next steps. If you are the incumbent, you know the background of the whole management team, and you also know their strengths and weaknesses. If you are new to the company, then close observation of how people react will give you an indication of their willingness to accept change.

Remember that, for today, you're just making observations. As you develop a clear sense of who is with you, you'll also see that there are hidden gems in the company that you'll uncover through further observation of their attitude and the work that they accomplish. The best example of this was the lady who became my production manager for a company I'd acquired in Belgium. She was doing what seemed like clerical work when I bought the company. Watching the number of people asking Miriam questions, it became very obvious that she was the leader who had all the information and answers to production questions. There will be more about Miriam in Step 4. For now, it's important to know that in every company there are hidden gems like Miriam waiting to be noticed.

A first step is to see who stands out in the initial meeting. At this point you're doing a rapid assessment so you have to learn to see things that other people don't tend to see. Nonverbal communication alone is very telling. Who sits where? How do they sit? Do they slump in their chair? Do they bring something on which to take notes? Pay attention to these details. They're likely the first signals of who is with you and who is not.

Your initial leadership is a lonely position but it will soon become obvious which other team members you can rely on to help advocate for the changes that you will be implementing. I have found this to be a very natural process if the person who is the catalyst for change provides a safe harbor for the people to join his team. The job of the leader is to create this sense of security and optimism that gives everyone confidence that the recovery vision is not only possible but also imminent. The leader's confidence must be real and not just glib Pollyanna pronouncements.

People's reaction to you gives a very good indication of whether they believe there is even a future for the company.

There are the natural Jeremiahs who constantly point out the next potential for disaster. At the other extreme are people who enthusiastically agree with everything you say. Both are equally dangerous. Well-thought-out alternatives to your plans should always be considered, especially if they are presented in a cogent convincing way. Observation skills and learning to rapidly read the room are key attributes of a leader.

Those who are not with you often self-identify incredibly quickly. I wish those people well and bid them adieu with the sentiment conveyed in the St. Crispin's Day speech from Shakespeare's *Henry V*: "That he which hath no stomach to this fight, / Let him depart; his passport shall be made."

EXCERPT FROM THE ST. CRISPIN'S DAY SPEECH FROM *HENRY V* BY WILLIAM SHAKESPEARE

That he which hath no stomach to this fight,
Let him depart; his passport shall be made
And crowns for convoy put into his purse:
We would not die in that man's company
That fears his fellowship to die with us.
This day is called the feast of Crispian:
He that outlives this day, and comes safe home,
Will stand a tip-toe when the day is named,
And rouse him at the name of Crispian.
He that shall live this day, and see old age,
Will yearly on the vigil feast his neighbours,

And say 'To-morrow is Saint Crispian:'
Then will he strip his sleeve and show his scars.
And say 'These wounds I had on Crispin's day.'
Old men forget: yet all shall be forgot,
But he'll remember with advantages
What feats he did that day: then shall our names.
Familiar in his mouth as household words
Harry the king, Bedford and Exeter,
Warwick and Talbot, Salisbury and Gloucester,
Be in their flowing cups freshly remember'd.
This story shall the good man teach his son;
And Crispin Crispian shall ne'er go by,
From this day to the ending of the world,
But we in it shall be remember'd;
We few, we happy few, we band of brothers;
For he to-day that sheds his blood with me
Shall be my brother; be he ne'er so vile,
This day shall gentle his condition:
And gentlemen in England now a-bed
Shall think themselves accursed they were not here,
And hold their manhoods cheap whiles any speaks
That fought with us upon Saint Crispin's day.

DO THE UNEXPECTED: PICK A JOB NOBODY ELSE WILL DO

I mentioned earlier that doing the unexpected allows you to control the narrative of the turnaround. This works when you're trying to uncover foul play, but it's also powerful for building trust and showing your employees that you're there to do the hard work that's required to revive the company.

One of the easiest ways to show your values as a leader is to have a real job. Unfortunately, most CEOs have lost touch with the coal face and have very little idea what is actually happening at the sharp end of the company. Find what you think is the least enjoyable job and select that as your job for the next few days.

When my daughter was in second grade, she was asked what her father did for a job. She told her teacher, "My dad doesn't do anything. He just tells other people what to do." You need to avoid this characterization of your leadership.

In the television series *Undercover Boss*, bosses disguise themselves and pretend to be a new employee to find out what is going on in their company. You obviously can't do this but you can show that there is no job in the company you are unwilling to do.

In a later chapter we talk about building a barn in a day, but here's an early glimpse at what happened in a company I had bought in Scotland. I asked the works committee (unofficial union) to select the worst cleanup job they could find for me during our three-day renovation of the factory. They chose one that had been neglected for over ten years. This was their litmus test to see whether or not I was a legitimate leader. They were convinced I would back down and delegate it to someone else.

The company made computer cabinets for all the major computer manufacturers in an area in Scotland called Silicon

Glenn, obviously a takeoff on Silicon Valley. The raw material for these cabinets was a giant rolled steel coil that was fed
into a 50-ton press. The pieces that were not the final stamped
parts fell into a giant pit in the ground approximately six feet
deep. The steel was lubricated with oil prior to stamping, and
over the years, the pit had become a fetid and toxic dump. It
had also been used as a general dumping ground for uneaten
lunches and worse. The smell was almost overpowering and
was a compelling reason why no one had ever started to clean
it out. As the new owner of the company, I had to show that
there was no cleanup job that I would not do. So I asked the
works committee to get me extra-large overalls, strong gloves,
and a mask, and I got to work.

It took three days of the hardest physical work I have ever
done, but after three days in the pit, the stamping press and
the pit were spotless. I had removed over 3,000 pounds of tangled metal coil. Everyone was surprised, but it earned me new
respect from the shop floor and immediately started changing
people's attitude towards me.

I talk more about building a barn in a day in Step 5. For
now, this story helps illustrate the importance of creating a
new impression. In my experience, many CEOs have no idea
how hard their employees work, so selecting a difficult job to
do in your own company sends a very effective message and
is a great self-teaching moment. It also helps you appreciate
what the front-line employees have to put up with every day
in order to complete their jobs. It is eye-opening to realize

what employees actually do and how they do their jobs, but most importantly, it sends the right message when undertaking a turnaround.

YOUR FIRST ONE-ON-ONE MEETING: THE CFO

Step 2 is dedicated to a deep-dive meeting into the company financials with the CFO. At this point, you're simply meeting to assess the CFO's leadership. You're getting a sense of whether they'll be an active strategist in the turnaround, or whether they're willing at all to participate in it.

To start, you need to find out how the CFO spends their time. CFOs traditionally spend a considerable amount of time both making the books look as good as they can be and making sure they adhere to Generally Accepted Accounting Principles (GAAP). Both these items distract from the leader's true mission, which is to find out how bad things are and how they can be improved in the future. The leader needs to understand and not delegate this vital part of the business.

With the enormous improvement in technology and software, it is fair to ask what the CFO does with their day. In the past there were a lot of numbers that had to be added by hand. Now all this is done for you instantly, including production of financial statements. So, what exactly does the CFO do?

There is a very simple way to find out. First, ask what they think are the five major tasks they need to accomplish to effectively do their job. When they have given you the list, ask them to keep track of the hours they spend on each task each day. They must fully distribute all the hours they work, i.e., at least eight hours a day. At the end of the week, you will have the total number of hours spent on each of the five tasks. These can be charted in a pareto chart (see example below) that easily identifies which takes the most time. This can lead to some very interesting discussions about what they are spending their time on and why a particular task takes so long.

Step 1 Pareto Chart

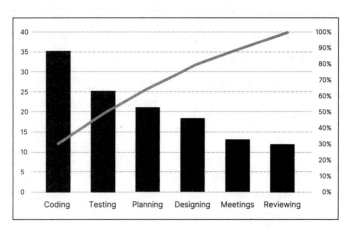

Tasks

PROBLEM AREA	OCCURRENCES	PERCENT OF TOTAL	CUMULATIVE PERCENT
Coding	35	28.23%	28.23%
Testing	25	20.16%	48.39%
Planning	21	16.94%	65.32%
Designing	18	14.52%	79.84%
Meetings	13	10.48%	90.32%
Reviewing	12	9.68%	100.00%

The effectiveness of this approach becomes very obvious very quickly. The CFO is normally one of the highest paid positions in a company, so it is important to quickly establish their value add. Many CFOs want to be financial journalists who just present you with the bad news about the previous month. On Day 1, you need to establish that they are a critical member of the leadership team and their role is as an executive not a journalist. They need to take the minimum amount of time preparing the financial statements and the maximum amount of time making recommendations on how to improve the financial status of the company. Many CFOs are more comfortable in the journalist role because that gives them an alibi and little or no responsibility for the financial outcome of the company.

The revelation can be very confrontational sometimes, and I have had a few CFOs just walk out. This never resulted in any upheavals but frequently revealed how little contribution they were actually making. If they refuse to let you know what they do—which again has happened to me—then you know you have found out something important on Day 1.

YOUR NEXT ONE-ON-ONE: THE COMPANY HISTORIAN

One last task on the first day is to ask to meet the employee who has been at the company the longest. Make sure you meet them in their work area and find somewhere to chat comfortably about the company. They are the company historian and, in many cases, know exactly what the challenges are firsthand. They can also tell you when the company was fun to work for and what caused it to go wrong.

In my second major turnaround, I tried this strategy on the first day and was stunned when the employee who had worked in the warehouse for over forty years pulled out a well-worn notebook. In it, he described exactly where the company had gone wrong. He outlined all the products that didn't sell—he knew because he had to move them up, down, and around the warehouse multiple times to try to hide them. He knew exactly when the company started its decline and provided me with a historical litany of disasters that caused the current financial problems. What a treasure trove of information on Day 1.

Long-standing employees have often become cynical because nobody has listened to them for so long. When you create the sort of listening environment I advocate, it creates a platform for them to communicate and finally share their story. I've found, 100% of the time that I've spoken with the employee who has been with the company the longest, that they produce an absolute wealth of information. People often ask me how I could know so much about a company at the end of Day 1. That's my secret: I went to the person who had the most knowledge, and they gave me insight that nobody else could give me.

DAY 1 RECAP

- If you are the current CEO, Day 1 needs to be demonstrably different from your normal routine. Change your demeanor, tone, and outlook so that employees know a new day is here. Take accountability for past mistakes and own your responsibility to make things right.

- Make physical changes in the office that encourage a collaborative environment. Your goals with these changes are to level the playing field, establish trust, and convey confidence, humility, and empathy.

- Do the unexpected. It's important that you do the managing and don't get managed by the employees because everything you do is expected and predictable.

- By the end of Day 1, you have **met with current company leaders** to share the new vision; selected a job in the company that you will do for the next few days; **met with the CFO** or the accountant to outline your expectations and have an initial indication of how deep the financial problems are; and **met with the employee who has been with the company the longest** to uncover a wealth of information about the company's situation.

- Moving forward, remember that you need to provide constant reassurance by frequently giving examples of all the changes that are starting to take effect. In a company I acquired in Scotland, we would stop the manufacturing process once a month to bring in a new piece of equipment. I would explain why it was purchased and the benefit that it was going to provide the company. This became a positive expectation every month and something everyone looked forward to. It also showed a new respect for everyone on the shop floor. No longer did they have to work with dilapidated old equipment. Instead, they could work with pride operating state-of-the-art equipment.

STEP 2

FINANCIAL AND CASH ASSESSMENT

If your CFO did not jump ship after your Step 1 meeting with them, you can now get to the important work of finding out what is really happening with the company financials. If the CFO did walk out—rare, but it happens—this early departure is never as bad as it seems. In the two or three times that it has happened to me, I found out that the person who reported to the CFO was actually doing the bulk of the accounting work and was all too eager to throw the recently departed CFO under the bus. If that's the case, you can work closely with that person to get to the heart of the company's financial situation.

Creating an accurate picture of the company's financial problems is essential to get moving in the right direction. This is your focus for Step 2. If you have a chance to review the current and previous year's financial statements prior to starting the turnaround assignment, you can get a head start on this process. Given the critical nature of most companies that are having financial problems, speed is of the essence. Your goal with this step is to uncover where and why the financial troubles exist and make a simple plan to solve each issue. You do not have the time to go back and change direction if something new is unearthed later. You just have to make a plan, stick to it, and pivot as needed.

WHY THE NUMBERS LOOK SO COMPLICATED

Before you start, take a deep breath, relax, and understand that company financials are ultimately addition and subtraction. No multiplication, no division, and no calculus required. So, for all the math phobics out there, you'll be relieved to know the necessary financial capability should have been comfortably mastered in kindergarten. With an Excel spreadsheet even the addition and subtraction are done for you. Ignore the entreaties from your CFO or accountant that it's more complicated than it looks. It is not. By the end of Step 2 you will feel a lot more comfortable with the entire subject of accounting.

Financial areas of a company are frequently very intimidating for both insiders and outsiders. Without being too cynical, I believe this is intentional. It helps avoid the true financial state and allows companies to kick the can down the road.

There are no stupid questions that can be asked when it comes to understanding financial statements. It's important to go through them line by line until you fully comprehend the exact nature of the company's financial condition. It also helps to be familiar with terms that are commonly used in the accounting arena, which you'll find in the glossary on page 221. Ask lots of questions, and if you don't understand something, keep asking until you do.

Your task in Step 2 is to simplify the company's financials as much as possible, but before we do that, it helps to understand why they tend to be so complicated in the first place.

Running a company's financials is a task delegated to the accounting department run by a CFO or a controller. Their traditional assignment is to make the company look as good as it can look. Rarely are financial statements accurate because there are compelling reasons to make sure they reflect only the most positive interpretation. This is particularly evident in companies having financial problems because it can cover over the cracks for quite a long time. In many cases the main driver for the deception is the bank, which I talk about in more detail later. Reviewing the bank agreements and covenants can give you a good idea of why the financial statements are overstated. It is far easier to massage the numbers than to take the hard actions required to bring a company into compliance with bank covenants. For readers who are not familiar with bank covenants, they are contractual agreements with the bank to maintain certain financial ratios that show the bank that you always have the ability to pay back your loan. This reporting is done on a monthly basis and the consequences of not meeting these numbers are serious. They can precipitate default interest rates, which in some cases could mean your interest rates almost doubling. This one has always puzzled me a little bit: if the company is struggling to meet its current payments, it does not make any sense to make payments even more difficult by charging more interest. Reflecting a sentiment attributed to Mark Twain, the banks' view is, "Don't tell me about the return on my money but the return of my money."

When you add to this the pressure from external shareholders and partners, it is very easy to understand why many companies embellish or outright misrepresent their financial condition. The idea that the numbers are the numbers suddenly becomes more opaque, adjustments are made month to month to absorb monthly variances, and deferrals and accruals further distort the actual picture. The problem is that once this has started, the numbers get further and further away from the true financial position.

CFOs and accountants are put in the unenviable position of having to use every accounting trick to make the numbers meet the expectations of the stakeholders. They also constantly remind themselves that they have a professional qualification to uphold, hence the dilemma. Do I present the numbers in the most accurate way or do I use all the legitimate accounting tricks to please the stakeholders? Rather than just present the numbers, everything is made more complicated. It is so complicated that only a professionally trained person can understand. The CFO has to consult with an outside accounting firm because there are areas that even they can't understand.

So here, right at the heart of the business, is this impenetrable area that seems to be written in a foreign language. Nothing is final and all the numbers seem like moving targets. Accruals, deferrals, prepaids, GAAP, FASB (Financial Accounting Standards Board). Compounding this are multiple sets of accounting books: Book Books, Tax Books, and other books. These spawn complex book-to-tax reconciliations because of significant differences between the two.

It is easy to understand why any sane person would steer far clear of this impenetrable accounting swamp. *But*—if you don't take the time to confront and understand the finances, it is impossible to plot the path to recovery.

TIME TO DIG INTO THE NUMBERS

Cash is the lifeblood of a company, so your first step towards figuring out what's going on is to ask your CFO or accountant to redo the books on a cash basis. Ask them to take out all the adjustments and just put together a spreadsheet. In many ways this will be a big relief to the CFO. This is something they have wanted to do for a long time but have been discouraged from doing because of the impact it would have on the stakeholders. With this kind of confessional, you will be shocked at all the details revealed to you by the CFO seeking absolution. During my many years doing turnaround work, I was always amazed at the speed and desire of CFOs to tell the truth when they had the prospect of a safe landing. In almost all cases the CFO knew the house was on fire, and finally the fire service has arrived to put out the fire. This is a complete relief for the CFO who no longer has to pretend that there is no fire.

Once the books are set to a cash basis, have the accountant simplify them into a spreadsheet starting with a basic **profit and loss statement** (see sample on page 77). The other key financial document is the **balance sheet**. This is really the main treasure trove of valuable information and the best indication of the depth of the problems.

With these reports in hand, you can ask fundamental questions about how much cash went out and how much cash came in on a daily basis. This very rapidly gives you an understanding of the cash flow of the company, something not reflected in the financial statements. During a turnaround situation, questions to confirm cash out, cash in, and current balance need to be asked every day.

Very soon you will be asking for projections: what cash do we expect to come in next week on a day-by-day basis and what cash do we expect to go out next week on a daily basis? There will be a great temptation for your accounting department to hedge their bets. Now is the time to demand complete transparency.

It is also a time to restrict outgoing cash so it is always less than the cash coming in. By default, this simple process produces positive cash flow even if the company is not profitable

Sample profit and loss statement

First six months	Jan	Feb	Mar	Apr	May	June	Total	%
Sales	$120,000	$ 135,000	$ 165,000	$ 180,000	$ 180,000	$ 184,000	$ 964,000	100%
Materials	$ 18,000	$ 20,250	$ 24,750	$ 27,000	$ 27,000	$ 27,600	$ 144,600	15%
Direct Labor	$ 30,000	$ 33,750	$ 41,250	$ 45,000	$ 45,000	$ 46,000	$ 241,000	25%
Gross margin	$ 72,000	$ 81,000	$ 91,000	$ 108,000	$ 108,000	$ 110,400	$ 578,400	60%
Expenses								
Salaries and benefits	$ 35,000	$ 35,000	$ 45,000	$ 50,000	$ 50,000	$ 50,000	$ 265,000	27%
Rent	$ 9,000	$ 9,000	$ 9,000	$ 9,000	$ 9,000	$ 9,000	$ 54,000	6%
Equipment lease	$ 25,000	$ 25,000	$ 25,000	$ 25,000	$ 25,000	$ 25,000	$ 150,000	16%
Utilities	$ 500	$ 500	$ 500	$ 500	$ 1,000	$ 1,000	$ 4,000	0%
Consumables	$ 3,000	$ 3,000	$ 3,000	$ 4,000	$ 4,000	$ 4,000	$ 22,500	2%
Misc	$ 1,250	$ 1,250	$ 1,250	$ 1,250	$ 1,250	$ 1,250	$ 7,500	1%
Total expenses	$ 74,250	$ 74,250	$ 84,250	$ 89,750	$ 90,250	$ 90,250	$ 503,000	52%
Profit	(2,250)	$ 6,750	$ 14,750	$ 18,250	$ 17,750	$ 20,150	$ 75,400	8%

at the time. It also highlights where the money is coming from and where it is going. This primary building block requires no financial expertise at all; it simply requires asking fundamental questions. Its value is in the fact that there is no interpretation required. As the owner of a small retail store will tell you: it is what is in the till that counts.

The accounting term for what I'm describing here is **source and application of funds**. It's a quick way of describing where the money is coming from and where it's going.

This is accounting at its simplest and most confrontational because it is what it is. So while you are trying to understand all the strange financial terms, don't get distracted from the most valuable information that is readily available: the daily cash flow. Also, this is a good time to request a detailed rationale for every payment; it will give you a very good early indication of financial leakages.

FIND OUT WHERE THE BODIES ARE BURIED

A primary task in Step 2 is to recalibrate the financial numbers to where they should have been all along. A recovery cannot begin if the starting point is not accurate. The big question is how to get to the bottom of the financial numbers quickly. Luckily, the numbers did not just appear. There is one person who should know what the true numbers are: the person who has been pressured into making them look as good as they can be.

The best way to get the accurate financial numbers is to assume the numbers are inflated. I always used a totally arbitrary 25% reduction in net worth of the company to start the process going. This gave the CFO a cushion to work with to make the necessary adjustments, thereby frequently revealing items that had been overvalued in the assets and liabilities that have been artificially reduced. Over the years my 25% guess turned out to be quite accurate. This can be a placeholder to extrapolate the impact on the company and the bank when the numbers are confirmed.

From here, you need to dig in and find out *where* the numbers are off, and why.

Fortunately, there are only a few places where the bodies can be buried. The easiest place is in inventory. This is because of the complexity that accountants and tax authorities have created in coming up with inventory's value. Inventory is also the hardest place to find discrepancies. The appendix describes all the challenges faced when trying to calculate the value of inventory. Suffice to say, fifty years in business and I have never seen a company that undervalued inventory. At this stage, the reduced value of the inventory is an estimate. But it should be reduced until the value is independently confirmed by actual physical counts and correct valuation of the inventory.

The other two places where adjustments are frequently made are in the **accounts receivable** (money that you are owed) and **accounts payable** (money that you owe).

Accounts Receivable

With accounts receivable you need to confirm that all the companies that owe you money have the capability and are willing to pay you. If not, an adjustment needs to be made and the receivable placed in the category of doubtful accounts. There is frequently great reluctance to do this because the money that the company has borrowed from the bank is an advance based on the accounts receivable. The banks require monthly reporting that indicates any potential doubtful accounts. Unfortunately, admitting that there are doubtful accounts then requires the company to immediately repay 100% of the amount that they have borrowed against that receivable. You can see from this the obvious reluctance to precipitate a financial crisis and a confrontation with the organization that is providing you with liquidity. And, therefore, the great temptation to overstate the value of receivables. The same overstatement applies to inventory because frequently the bank uses inventory valuation as a calculation of what they're willing to lend. Bank borrowing can rapidly become the tail that wags the dog.

Accounts Payable

There is a very easy way to understate your accounts payable: don't book the payable invoices and leave them in a drawer or folder. I have frequently found this phenomenon, and it is an early symptom of denial. If the payable invoices are not in their books, the owners feel they can get a temporary respite from the doom they know is coming their way. I have seen intelligent owners and CFOs display this basic form of denial. At one company I worked with many years ago, the CEO's top drawer was filled with invoices. This very bright man, who had a master's in psychology from MIT, did not want to face the truth. Hiding the invoices was his last-ditch stand to make the company financials look better than they were.

ONE FINAL PLACE I have found it worthwhile to look for buried bodies is in the accounting files for professional services. Here you will find all the bills for legal and accounting services. This can be very revealing as it shows any outstanding or previous litigation, or any tax issues that required engaging an accounting firm to resolve.

VERIFY EVERYTHING

Demand absolute irrefutable proof of every line item in the balance sheet. On rare occasions, when confronted with the inevitable, the CFO will pack their bags and walk out. They know the jig is up and do not want to face the consequences. This is a rare occurrence and gives you absolute confirmation that the books are rigged. Like I said, if you find yourself in this situation, there is usually someone else in the company who is very familiar with the company financials.

Verification of the numbers is supposed to be done by outside auditors, but as you will see from their engagement letter, they are only responsible for the numbers they are given and take no responsibility for their accuracy. They will, however, make sure that the numbers they are given are correctly presented from an accounting standpoint and meet GAAP. If all auditors' reports truly reflected the financial state of a company, then it would not be possible to have an Enron, FTX, or Silicon Valley Bank.

As part of Step 2 you have to be the super auditor, and the financial Inspector Clouseau. Look for clues, don't trust anything, and verify everything. There is a fancy name for this process: forensic accounting. You will find it very easy to do this task if you take every line item in the profit and loss statement and the balance sheet and keep asking questions until you're fully satisfied that they accurately reflect the numbers that are in the financial statements.

Make no assumptions. It is even good practice to go as far as verifying the existence of all employees. One of the companies I was working with had a number of employees who were hired solely for extracurricular activities. The owner of the company fancied himself a latter-day Don Juan and had created a marketing department full of attractive young ladies. Each had their apartment and living expenses covered by the company—expensed under various categories of rent and entertainment. The latter was probably one of the few that accurately represented what funds were being spent on. It was only when I demanded that all employees attend a company meeting that I finally got to meet the beautiful ladies from the marketing department. Needless to say, they were early casualties in the employee reductions that took place soon after. I did, however, feel they were significantly underpaid for the job they were asked to do.

CREATING YOUR FINANCIAL PLAN AND BUDGET

Once you've gone through the forensic accounting phase, it's time to put together your go-forward financial plan and budget. Above all, keep it simple and be realistic. Cyberspace is full of business plans that could never be achieved. The following are some key considerations to keep in mind as you put together your plan.

Never Budget for a Loss; Only Budget for a Profit

Companies that budget for a loss achieve exactly that. It is more comfortable to budget for a loss because that allows you to kick the can down the road and avoid the hard decisions you have to make, but planning to run a company at a loss is not running a company.

Just before I bought a manufacturing company from its parent company in Belgium, I was shown the projections that had been shared with the board of directors. The chart was quite simple: it showed a loss of $1 million in the current year, breakeven the following year, and a significant profit in the third year. Although the turnaround was going to take a year, the chart was at least an attempt to get to profitability. It was then that a board member dropped the other shoe. This subsidiary had been using the same chart for the last nine years, accumulating a 9-million-euro loss.

My recommendation is to create a budget that produces a profit in thirty days. This forces you to face the tough questions immediately. Start with the most realistic and pessimistic sales projections. For example: If the sales projections are $1 million, then sequester a minimum 10% profit at the bottom of the projections. Now you have automatically limited your spending budget to $900,000.

Reduce the Number of Expense Categories

Most expenditures are relatively fixed, such as rent, utilities, etc. The biggest variable is always payroll, and it is also the quickest and easiest to change. Reducing payroll has an immediate impact on profitability and cash flow.

From the projections you need to come up with a payroll cost you can afford, not how much your payroll currently costs. Once you have decided how much you can afford, then you need to decide the makeup of the personnel you are going to keep. This is discussed in more detail in Step 4. At this point, we are at the budgeting stage so all we need is a number. Later on, we can decide who and how many. For budgeting purposes, we just need a number for each main category of employees. In a manufacturing company, you have direct employees (people who actually produce product on the shop floor) and indirect employees (people who support direct employees on the shop floor, like inspectors, supervisors, planners, etc.). The final employee group is administration, which includes sales, marketing, accounting, clerical and IT and the executives. Amounts filled in on the spreadsheet will identify what you can afford for each of these categories.

Cancel Overtime

Once you have a clear idea what the company can afford moving forward, ask the CFO or accountant to create a spreadsheet of the budget for the next twelve months. One caution: do not include a budget for overtime. Overtime is one of those insidious line items that is virtually impossible to control. It is very hard to determine how long any given job should take, but you can rest assured that prior to your arrival, overtime was used to increase an employee's pay as a way of retaining them without actually giving them a pay raise. It may mean that you have to increase people's pay to keep them but at least you will have a fixed amount that you can budget for. Overtime is also never costed into a customer price quote so a profitable job can be made unprofitable because of overtime. The most diligent seeming employee can be the one who is taking the most advantage of overtime pay. You only have to look at lifeguards at beaches or police departments in California to see people making over $300,000 a year in overtime work. New York State paid out more than $1.36 billion in overtime in 2022.* I have found over the last forty years that overtime is one of the most insidious financial leakages in a company. The simple way to stop it is to notify all employees that there will be no approved or unapproved overtime.

Make sure that everyone is notified. Given some of the more litigious states, it is possible for employees to go back

---

* See: https://www.osc.ny.gov/files/reports/pdf/cy2022-overtime-report.pdf

many years to claim overtime pay that they had not been paid. Many years ago, I had an employee in a shipping department who always stayed late in his office and read the newspaper. When he was let go, he tried to claim that he was working overtime and needed to be paid. A simple declaration that there is no overtime moving forward is the best way to eliminate these types of issues.

WHEN YOU REACH the end of Step 2, it's a good time to reflect back on how much you have learned about the company so far. This should give you added energy and confidence to complete the next eight steps. You will also be surprised how quickly these steps can be taken and how enjoyable it is to start getting control of a runaway train.

STEP 3

COMPANY MEETINGS

Step 3 is a major milestone because it's the first time you reveal the turnaround plan to the whole company. Up to this point, your work with Steps 1 and 2 has been behind the scenes with department leaders. Now, you're taking your first step into the future as you start to show employees that a new day has come. Things are finally going to start getting brighter.

Company meetings are your chance to get everyone's input and ideas as well as assess who should be on the turnaround team. Small things like turning up on time, where a person sits, how they sit, or whether they look happy are key observations to the go-forward plan of selecting the final team. It is essential that only people who want to be on the team make the final cut.

Meetings should start and end with an upbeat vision of the future. In the middle, the turn around leader needs to communicate the seriousness of the mission. This sandwich approach convinces everyone that it's getting brighter and there's no chance of returning to the dark old days. This is a new beginning.

Everyone's suggestions must be documented and published publicly throughout the company, with a commitment to a specific implementation date. Once you do this, you'll notice the company's energy and momentum change very quickly. The publication of the employee recommendations shows not only that you are listening but also that you value employee input. And once people know you're listening, they will come to you with further recommendations and be more deeply engaged in the turnaround process.

A METHOD FOR EFFECTIVE COMPANY MEETINGS

When organizing employee meetings, it is important for the moderator to create a good ambiance with the participants. You're trying to get the maximum amount of information possible in the shortest amount of time, and I have a specific method to make these meetings as effective as possible. These are the key parameters:

- **Have no more than ten people in each meeting and cap each meeting at one hour**. This ensures that everyone has a voice in the meeting while keeping it a reasonable length. This group size also gives you a chance to notice the interactions between attendees. Careful observation can tell you a lot about who should be on the team going forward.

- **Never put someone in a meeting with their direct supervisor**. This ensures that input isn't limited by fear of retribution.

- **Have a mix of as many different departments and job categories as possible in each meeting**. This brings people out of their silos and opens up their perspective. Bring together employees from the warehouse with those from administrative offices. Give them a chance to be in conversation, hear one another, and learn how their work affects their colleagues. This may be the first time that they have ever met some of the people in the group. Most people leave these meetings with a greater appreciation for what other employees do, and in many cases, what they had to put up with came as a big surprise.

- **Instruct everyone to come prepared with at least one recommendation that they feel would improve their job**. You want to hear from everyone. Anyone who does not show up with a recommendation is likely signaling to you that they are not a willing participant in the turnaround.

- **Have one designated person who documents the recommendations**. If need be, they can follow up after the meeting to get more detail and clarity on the specific recommendations to make sure they are properly described for implementation.

These meetings give you a ringside seat to observe enthusiasm and participation. Once the group is assembled, a simple starting point is to ask each employee, "What is one thing that annoys you most when you come to work?" Many people will be shocked that they've even been asked. This will reveal a major item that causes antagonism every day. Removing these items can have a very positive effect on overall morale.

The true litmus test is when attendees are asked, "What about your job do you enjoy most?" The most frequent reply is, "It's just a job." If there's nothing to enjoy about their job, they are unlikely to be a contributor to turning around the company.

I also ask attendees if they would be willing to take on a new job that involved a lot of hard work and learning something completely new but had significantly more pay. If the answer is no, then they have completed their self-assessment for you.

You'll find some employees don't want to participate, but as the leader, you need to find ways to help them participate. In my meetings I used to find the most shy and reticent person and sit them next to me on my right. When the meeting started, I would announce that they were sitting in the hot seat and would be the first person to offer a suggestion on how to improve their job. This always broke the ice and added a little humor to the meeting. I used to change the hot seat every meeting to keep everyone guessing which seat it would be.

Finally, remember to closely observe yourself in these meetings to make sure your leadership makes a good impression. Leadership is a constant and continuous process. If you have self-doubts, keep them to yourself. No one wants to see the captain inspecting the lifeboats. If you need to inspect them, do it at night when no one is watching. Smiling also denotes confidence. Everybody is watching you, and you are sending signals consciously and unconsciously all the time. Introducing some humor goes a long way to reduce the tension that is always present during financially difficult times in a company. This does not mean that you are not serious about the mission, but it does make you more human and easier to have confidence in. You are asking people in the company to change and to do things differently. Frequently, the way they've always done things is the way they have been instructed to do them. Your mission is to coax them back to a more effective way of doing their job and to make it more enjoyable for them to come to work.

REMIND EVERYONE THAT THEY'RE THERE BY CHOICE

Another direct question that frequently produces some interesting answers at these meetings is, "Why did you choose this job?" This often elicits stunned looks. In many cases they never really thought much about finding a job that they actually wanted and enjoyed. A lot of this attitude was inherited from previous eras when there was limited employment and limited growth in the economy. Employees were pleased to just find a job that paid on a regular basis so they could take care of their families. As discussed earlier, we are now living in an entirely different paradigm. This new paradigm will continue for many, many years and creates opportunities for work and for individual satisfaction in work.

The challenge is to convince employees that they have many options and that they have an obligation to themselves to find an opportunity where they can really enjoy work and gain personal satisfaction from it. Many people just drift into a job and avoid the care and scrutiny that should be applied to one of the most important decisions anybody makes in their life. If they get this decision correct, they will not only be blessed with immense satisfaction but also frequently become very successful at their chosen occupation.

During the meetings you need to emphasize that the employees are their own agents and can determine their own destiny. They have the autonomy to improve and enhance their jobs; they do not have to raise their hand in class to ask permission. The light often suddenly goes on during the meeting: not only do they have permission to voice their opinions but also those opinions are being actively solicited.

I always mention that there are only two decisions that determine genuine happiness in life: choosing the right spouse and choosing the right job. It has always amazed me how little care people take in these momentous decisions that have such an enormous impact on their life. There is always a revelation that maybe they do have control of their destiny and that they can change the future for their own benefit rather than hope someone will do it for them.

We are obsessed with the idea that we should never make people uncomfortable. It's the lack of comfort that can act as a great stimulus to try something new. The new economy is going to have more jobs than people for many years. By encouraging people to find a job that they enjoy more is hardly hurtful or unkind. Instead, by encouraging them to change, you are doing them a great service.

Many years ago, I had a friend who was a doctor, and over dinner one night, he expressed how depressed he was being a doctor. He did not enjoy being around sick people every day. He had an optimistic outgoing personality and the idea that the rest of his life would be spent around people who were ill, depressed him immensely. I asked him, if he had a choice, what would he really choose to do. He told me his parents wanted him to be a doctor like his father so he studied hard, went to university, and became a doctor. Now he was in his mid-thirties, trapped doing something that was well paying and respected by the community but that he disliked intensely. What he really wanted was to be a pilot. He'd always loved airplanes and had a genuine passion for flying.

During dinner I told him he was in a unique position to do what he wanted to do. Learning to fly is very expensive and the reason it takes a long time to become a pilot is because of the cost. This was not a constraint for him. He could go down to Phoenix, Arizona, and fly six to eight hours a day and very quickly qualify as a commercial pilot. After a brief pause, he said that's what he was going to do. And he did it. Unfortunately, we lost touch but I'm convinced that he followed through and became a commercial pilot. Whenever I think about that conversation with my friend, I have this interesting vision that one day he will be flying and a flight attendant will tell him one of the passengers is seriously ill and they need to ask over the intercom if there is a doctor on board. He will of course respond that he is also a doctor, which will surprise not only the crew but also the passengers.

Getting employees to realize they have lots of choices is very difficult. There is a Stockholm syndrome in employment that convinces employees not only that they are kidnapped but also that their captors are benevolent and have their best interest at heart. It is important to give employees choices and not assume that they are content with their current work assignment. Giving people the choice initially to stay, go, or consider a job change within the company can create a new freedom. You must establish this early on because you need everyone enthusiastically rowing in the right direction at this critical time in the turnaround.

PUBLICATION OF EMPLOYEE RECOMMENDATIONS

Create a detailed publication of the future vision that incorporates employee recommendations. Include in the publication the dates when changes will be made and communicate with all employees once the changes have been implemented. It is very important that dates are met. If they are not, the reason needs to be shared and a new date given to the person who made the suggestion. Your credibility as a leader is at stake and everyone is watching. Make sure you follow Babe Ruth's example: if you point to stands, make sure you hit the ball there.

You can revisit the company meeting scenario on a quarterly basis. Repeating the process gains additional momentum when the initial steps have been completed. The main purpose is to show all employees that individually they have power to make and recommend changes. In many cases this is the first time that employees have been asked how the company can make their job more enjoyable. I have found a number of very fully engaged employees through these meetings. Although it can end up being more of a vent session, when employees know that their requests will be implemented, they feel genuinely empowered and the meeting takes on an optimistic direction.

This is asking people not just what they don't like but what they would like to change and improve—and what makes them annoyed every time they come to work. I had an employee many years ago who just needed an extension cord. He had been asking for one for over a month and could not properly do his work without one. He survived by borrowing one from an employee close by, which stopped that employee being productive. The problem was solved when I visited the local Home Depot at lunchtime and bought five extension cords of various lengths plus a mat to prevent people tripping on them. Speedy resolution of the problem showed that there was a new sheriff in town and things were going to happen fast.

There will be genuine surprise when the employees see all the changes that are planned, and they will have a genuine sense of pride and ownership when their own suggestions are highlighted. All suggestions and recommendations need to have an author or authors to identify and acknowledge where each came from. If the company has one hundred employees, after ten meetings of ten employees, you will have a treasure trove of one hundred recommendations. Many of these will be small but will have a big impact on employee morale and the day-to-day work.

When I first implemented this process many years ago, once the employees got over being asked for their candid opinions, I was amazed at the quality of the suggestions. In the first company I worked with, everything had been top-down and no ideas were ever solicited from the employees. Simple queries about what annoyed them most when they came to work brought out deeper issues. One employee raised the issue of another employee always taking his torque wrench and other tools. Because he needed the torque wrench to do his job, he spent the first fifteen minutes of his day looking around the shop for the tool that had been taken from his area. When asked how he would resolve this problem, he said it was quite simple. There are only three areas in the manufacturing facility that need torque wrenches: the company needed to purchase two more torque wrenches and create shadow boxes to house all the tools needed for each area. At the end of the day, the employee in charge of that area was to confirm that all the tools had been placed in the appropriate shadow box. When this was implemented, the problem disappeared along with this employee's daily frustration. A further benefit was that the employee added fifteen minutes of productive work to his schedule every day.

When an item like this is multiplied by one hundred, the cumulative list of changes is very impactful. Publishing and sharing the list shows you listened; more importantly, it telegraphs your intention to follow through on employees' recommendations. In a number of cases, I have had requests from employees to repeat the process again in three months' time. The second time around, employees are even more creative and confident, and the quality of the suggestions improves even more. Having seen their previous ideas carried forward successfully, they trust that future recommendations will be received and implemented in the same way.

EMPLOYEE RETENTION TELLS ALL

Moving forward, make these meetings a normal part of your company's routine. After this initial round, all subsequent meetings are with the team members you've retained. Remember, though, no matter how carefully you select the right people in the company for your go-forward strategy, there are always a few boobirds left in the crowd. This small but vocal group are only too willing to remind everybody that they knew all along it wasn't going to work. You have to convince them that things have changed, but if they persist, they can become corrosive to the whole turnaround process. At that point you need to suggest they find a company they would enjoy working at more.

One of the most important metrics in business is employee turnover. A recent company that I have been involved with had 120 employees. When I asked how many W-2s (Wage and Tax Statement form) they had produced in the prior year, I was told they would get that number for me. The fact that they did not have that number at hand indicated to me that this was not an important metric to them. When I received the number, it was over 500. It was very obvious what one of the major problems was. Employees vote with their feet. High turnover, besides being expensive and exhausting, is probably one of the best predictors of a company's demise. One of the early signs that a company is truly on the mend is when the turnover drops. As a leader, it should be common practice for you to complete all exit interviews to find out why you have failed to provide the opportunities that the employee was looking for. In times of low unemployment, this is even more important. The loss of a single employee can have a major impact. It is also important to have an early visit with new employees: first, to ask them why they joined the company and, second, to share with them the vision of the company going forward. This is a CEO's function, not HR's. These employees work for you, not the HR department.

STEP 4

PERSONNEL ASSESSMENT

You'll likely complete your company meetings with a good sense of the people who will stay for the turnaround and who will leave. Now it's time for one of the most challenging steps: making the final selects for your go-forward team and letting everyone else go.

As we covered in Step 2, the first part of this process is to simply figure out a personnel budget that will make the company profitable again. Remember, during financial review, you're not thinking about *who* you would like to keep but *how much payroll the company can afford*. If your company currently has an annual payroll of $2 million and is losing money, you need to calculate the amount of payroll you can afford in order to make an immediate profit of 10%. Once you know the amount that will achieve your goal, you can select the team that meets that financial criterion.

There is a great temptation to justify keeping more people than you can afford. That creates a situation where additional people will have to be let go in the future. The process becomes death by a thousand cuts and employees learn to play defense to make sure their jobs are not cut in the future. You must reduce the team only once and do so aggressively. Once that difficult work is done, you can inform everyone that the cuts are done and this is the team, regardless of any further adverse financial conditions in the future. Explain that if further reductions are required to help the company survive, there will be a prorated reduction of compensation that will impact everyone equally. If these drastic steps are needed, it would send a positive message if senior management took an even higher percentage reduction, since they are in a better position to weather a financial storm. Awareness that everyone is being treated fairly will be the foundation of the company in the future.

I know it seems harsh, but with any company it is very dangerous to offer severance pay unless an employee has a specific contractual agreement that identifies severance pay. This is very rare in the industries I worked in but certainly should be honored if that is in the individual's contract. The cash you have left is the lifeblood of the company and is a scarce resource. It must only be used for the future survival of the company, not to salve your conscience about having to lay off people. I have seen grand gestures in severance pay become the final nail in the coffin when the company failed because it had eaten its last batch of seed corn. Your job is to keep the company alive at all costs. A profitable company in the future can always hire back good people who are let go. A company that has closed its doors cannot.

Once you've chosen your go-forward team, it's important to preserve the dignity of employees who did not make the cut. Be sure to thank those employees for their contribution and to let them know if the financial circumstances had been different, you would not have had to make such difficult decisions. It is also important to hold out a carrot—but no promises—that when the company returns to profitability there is a possibility that they will be rehired.

WHO ARE THE MARINES AND WHO IS IN THE FIFTH COLUMN?

In selecting who stays and who goes, I recommend looking at employees as falling into one of three main groups:

- Group 1: The Marines – 20%
- Group 2: The Ambivalent – 60%
- Group 3: The Fifth column – 20%

Each of the above groups normally self-identify at the company meetings in Step 3. Some will stay hidden for a while, but the fifth column always raise their heads over the parapet. Informing employees that the turnaround task will entail hard work helps identify the fifth column—and also the marines. The fifth column very rarely has any positive suggestions and frequently points out that everything was tried before and never worked.

It is vital to identify and extricate the fifth column as quickly as possible. The fifth column is actively trying to recruit the ambivalent group in the middle with a constant barrage of negative input along with disparagement of the company, its prospects, and fellow employees. They are corrosive cancers that will eat away at all your turnaround progress and need to be excised at the earliest opportunity. The marines are always too busy doing their job. When the fifth column is excised, the ambivalent will rapidly be inducted into the marines as there is now no other choice. The company momentum has now immediately shifted in your direction.

IDENTIFY THE INDISPENSABLE TEAM MEMBERS

The process of reducing your workforce is rarely simple. The fifth column is the easiest to extricate, but in many instances, you'll need to cut several more employees. When this is the case, I've found it very effective to ask each manager to rank everyone in their department. The ranking should be based on who you would miss the most if they did not work for you. The ranking should disregard their current position and should be based on criteria like energy, willingness to help others, and overall optimism. These people will be the key players in your go-forward strategy. They must believe passionately in the company's future and want to be an active part of it. Buy-in at this point is very indicative of the level of effort and enthusiasm that they will display in the future.

The largest reduction I ever had to do was from 480 employees to 240—and it needed to take place almost immediately. There was significant risk of not being able to meet payroll if the reductions were not made. This was genuinely a lifeboat drill. I brought together the heads of the twenty different departments in the boardroom and explained the challenges that the company was facing. Most of them were fully aware of how serious the situation was and asked how best they could help. I asked them to put together a list of all the employees in their department and then rank them (from one to ten, or however many people were in their department), not by seniority but by the employee who was least dispensable (#1) and the employee who was most dispensable (#10).

I then asked them to cancel any meetings they may have had for the next day and to meet me at a nearby hotel at seven o'clock in the morning with their lists. These they wrote on large pieces of paper that we posted on the walls around the conference room. The process was then quite straightforward, although it got a lot more difficult towards the end. The first thing I asked was for each head to please remove the person at the bottom of their list and indicate to me how that would impact their department. To my surprise there was very little concern about the impact of this first round of employee reductions. Unfortunately, we had eleven more rounds to go.

As you can probably appreciate, this got more difficult with every round, but I let everybody know that we were going to stay at the hotel until the task was completed. At two o'clock the following morning, we finally had the 240 people we needed to let go in order to save the company. We had complete agreement and unanimity from the department heads that the people we were keeping were the people they needed. Within four weeks the company had moved to positive cash flow and was well on its way to being turned around. As a postscript, forty years later the company that was close to bankruptcy was sold for over $600 million and had grown to over 1,500 employees. Those tough decisions around employee reduction saved the family business and enabled forty years of growth and prosperity that would otherwise never have existed.

QUESTION—AND CHALLENGE—EVERYTHING

There's still much to be done after you've identified your indispensable employees. One of your biggest tasks is to figure out what jobs the people you're keeping should do—and even what they should be paid.

This is the time during a turnaround that you need to be creative. Other than minimum wage, there is a limited set of rules regarding what you can pay. Giving yourself permission to be creative will help you come up with some elegant solutions that had likely never been entertained at the company before. Make no assumptions about people's skills or desire to do certain jobs; consolidate jobs; even increase compensation. The total payroll cannot exceed the budget, but there are very few parameters around how you can achieve this. This is also the time to do a deep dive into what individual employees actually do to determine any overlaps or consolidations that can be done.

Sometimes the simplest way to reduce costs is to counterintuitively increase pay. You can do this by having two people do the job that was previously done by three people and increasing their pay. Now the two people have an incentive to find more efficient ways of doing their work but they also get rewarded financially for doing it. This gets highlighted when you receive a request for an additional person in a department of three people. Pose the option to them of taking half the pay for this new person and sharing it with the current employees and then ask if that would work. Any time I've done this, the team unequivocally agreed that this would be the best solution. This revealed the general consensus that they did not want to increase their workload unless they were paid more. How many times in companies are people added to departments without asking the existing employees whether they would be willing to do the additional work for additional pay?

Research into employees' backgrounds can also reveal additional skill sets and, in some cases, a desire to do entirely different jobs. The best example of this is when I eliminated the inspection department in one company, only to find out that no one really enjoyed the job. They were only there because the pay rate in the inspection department was better than that of a shop-floor machinist. When I moved the sequestered inspectors back to the shop floor but maintained their inspector's pay, I instantly had a group of highly talented machinists who knew how to do the job well, genuinely enjoyed the job, and could mentor younger people. A huge win all round.

Question everything, including the value of seniority and experience. Just because someone has been working at a job for multiple years does not mean their experience becomes more valuable each year. For instance, if someone has learned and is competent in a specific skill and it took six months to become competent, if they apply that skill repeatedly and continuously for ten years, that additional time is not proportionately more valuable. I know this sounds a little harsh but I've seen many cases where a person's pay level is related to their number of years' experience. Whether that specific employee is actually worth more pay needs to be carefully balanced against an equally skilled employee with less experience who is paid less.

In a turnaround situation, it is very critical that you utilize funds as efficiently as possible. So, if someone with ten years' experience is getting paid significantly more than an equally competent person who has three years' experience, careful consideration must be taken to determine whether the higher payroll cost of one over the other is beneficial to the company. The same applies to seniority. If someone has been with the company for many years, should they be paid more than someone who has recently joined?

I have frequently been faced with the situation where an employee feels they are owed more because they have stayed with the company a long time. My question to the employee has always been: if another company had offered you significant higher compensation, would you have stayed? Most employees honestly tell me that they would not have stayed; they would have taken the new position. From this, I point out that both parties are free agents. Neither party owes the other party anything except to be treated with respect during the time both parties work together. There is no accumulated tenure every year; an employee has made the free choice to stay with the company.

Unions have always promoted seniority as a way of stratifying employees. When a company is experiencing financial difficulty, the entire employee structure needs to be reviewed. That is not to say there is no value in experience, but at some point, there is a limited amount of additional value gained from experience. Many years ago, in my first major turnaround, a leading beer and wine distributor, I had to implement a significant reduction in force: 50%—from 480 people to 240. The company was a union shop so there were added complexities of seniority, work rules, and more. The only way to approach this was to bring in the union at an early stage and offer to let the union's accountants review the books. The options were to either make the changes and retain some union jobs or lose all the business to a nonunion competitor. The choice was stark but we got full approval to work around all the union rules for six months. This allowed us to make employee choices in the company based on merit and not longevity and seniority, which were joined at the hip.

If you find yourself up against union rules, questioning and challenging everything can feel especially difficult—but it is possible to change even the most rigid practices. I have worked with a number of unions over the years, and when the financial situation is fully shared with them and an alignment of interests is established, their cooperation has been very productive. The most interesting situation was a company in Belgium that I bought where I had two unions. One was Catholic and the other, Protestant. When I first arrived at the company, I was completely unaware what a challenge this would be. The reason for the two unions was a peculiarity of Belgium. This tiny country has three languages: Flemish, French, and German. There is a fierce loyalty to the group that speaks your language. So, the battle lines were drawn with French/Catholic on one side and Flemish/Protestant on the other. Both unions despised the management and each other with equal venom.

The only way I could see to resolve this impasse was to have a summit meeting with both unions. Setting up the meeting was an impossible task until I hit on a fun way to make it work. How could I get them both to meet with me at the same time? I knew the Belgian weakness for fine food and wine, and although it was not a direct bribe, it was worth a try. My secretary Anelise found this wonderful restaurant in Liége near the factory. It had a months' long waiting list, but somehow she managed to get a reservation for three people. On the big night, both union bosses arrived at the same time. When they saw each other, they immediately turned around to leave.

I caught them just in time and then explained that the worst that could come from the evening was enjoyment of fine cuisine and wine. We sat down, and I immediately handed each the wine list and asked them to choose the finest wine on the list. Both were stunned initially and then promptly went into an earnest discussion about which year produced the best Petrus wine. They chose what they both felt was the best year, and without realizing it, this probably was the only thing they had ever agreed on. The sommelier was summoned, and with great fanfare the fine bottle of Petrus was opened. Waiters hovered around our table all night to view the spectacle that was unfolding. Soon a second bottle was ordered and the elaborate process of decanting was repeated. At the conclusion of the second bottle, all parties agreed to work for a common goal of saving the company and taking care of the employees. I still flinch when I think of the cost of two bottles of Petrus, but it was a very good investment and showed me that even the most intransigent enemies can be brought together if you can establish common ground.

Consider and challenge every constraint that may be getting in the way of you creating a team that will turn the company around. Just because something has always been done in a certain way is no reason to keep doing it that way. Usually, that kind of limited thinking is what got the company in a financial bind in the first place. You may be surprised to find that even the most seemingly rigid constraints are quite flexible when the company's life is on the line.

FIND THE HIDDEN GEMS

One of the true joys of turnaround work is to find hidden employee gems in some unexpected places. This can happen at any point during the turnaround, but sooner is always better so that you can have the most qualified people in each role. The most notable example of this was in the Belgian company that I've mentioned several times now. The company not only had financial problems but also significant operational problems. The latter were highlighted by an inability to deliver a product on time to their major customer, Airbus. The company was in the aerospace business where there is great sensitivity to on-time delivery. Most suppliers are single source, which means they are the only ones manufacturing a specific part number. Airplanes are one of the most complex products made, and if components do not arrive on time, the delivery date of the whole airplane is jeopardized. And that affects the airlines, who are the end customers and who are contractually entitled to compensation from the aircraft supplier if delivery is late.

One undelivered $50 part can delay a $200-million aircraft. This differential illustrates the stress that can be created by late deliveries.

So, it is not difficult to understand how much pressure is brought to bear on suppliers if they are not delivering their components on time. This was exactly the situation I faced after I had bought the company. They had missed the due date for virtually all the items that they had to deliver to Airbus. They were also in danger of losing many potentially lucrative contracts, which would have further compounded an already serious financial situation. The problem needed to be addressed immediately.

My glass-walled office in the company was in the corner of the production planning area. I could see not only all the employees in the production planning area but also the shop floor. In order to try to resolve the production problem, I called into my office the general manager whose overall responsibility was production. I asked him a few straightforward questions about some large orders that were late. He said it would take a while to get that information, but he would be back to me as soon as he could. (This should have been my first clue that something was amiss.)

From my office I watched how the whole process of getting information about this troublesome production played out. First the general manager went to the desk of the operations manager, who shook his head and went to the desk of the plant manager, who also shook his head and then went to the desk of another employee. Finally, they all ended up at the far end of the room. There sat a young woman who was diligently working on a computer terminal when the entourage arrived. She quickly entered a few key strokes and produced a printout that had all the production information I needed. The general manager triumphantly came into my office clutching the printout. He explained the reason for the late production was that the parts were not started on time. Why, I asked, did he not have a terminal on his desk so he could get this information every day and make sure the parts were started on time? He looked at me in horror. To start with, he said, he did not know how to use the computer, and secondly, it was not his job.

It became very obvious that the woman at the end of the room knew how to get all the information to make sure the components started on time, but she was the low person on the totem pole. Her job was just to provide information when asked, not to actually instigate any action with the information she obtained.

Miriam was the young lady at the end of the room and she was an absolute gem. She had enormous advantages over her supervisors. She had been an au pair in the UK and spoke perfect English. She was the only person who fully understood the MRP (material requirements planning) system. She had an incredible ability to remember the hundreds of part numbers that were on the manufacturing floor. She knew the most critical part of the planning: when to start the manufacturing process to make sure the components were completed on time. She was the perfect person to manage the entire production floor.

When I made the decision to promote Miriam to production manager there were gasps of horror among her male counterparts. She's just a clerk, I was told, and she's young and a woman. I tripled her pay, and almost miraculously, production was back on track by the end of her first month on the job. No one had asked Miriam's opinion on how to get the product manufactured on time when she was in a clerical position, but now that she had the authority to leverage her knowledge, there was no holding her back.

There are many Miriams in companies, just waiting to be found. Like an understudy in a Broadway play or a backup player in the NFL, they are waiting for a chance to show what they can do. The challenge is that sometimes they're hidden so deep in an organization that they're hard to find. In the employee meetings, keep a watchful eye for the Miriams. They are the people that everyone goes to for information. When given an opportunity to shine, they always exceed expectations. In the meetings they are frequently the ones that bring a notepad, pay keen attention, and ask penetrating questions. As said before, they are the ones that have the information that other people use.

USING THE PROCESS outlined in this chapter, you will be amazed at how quickly you are able to pick your go-forward team. Once decisions are made, it is important to get all the employees together and let them know how difficult the selection process was. As I mentioned in Step 1, I often explain this situation using the analogy of selecting a fifty-three-player NFL team from ninety training-season starters. It's not a negative reflection on the people who are let go. They simply did not make the team.

STEP 5

IMPLEMENTATION OF EMPLOYEE RECOMMENDATIONS

At this point in the turnaround, you've scaled down the team to your most critical members. You're also holding a wealth of recommendations from your employee meetings. Now, it's time to put this reenergized workforce into action and implement as many of those recommendations as possible, as quickly as possible.

Employee recommendations will look quite different from one industry to the next, but I've found that, almost universally, a great number of the suggestions have to do with improving the overall work environment. It is so critical to have a clean, organized, well-run workspace that everyone will be happy to go to every workday. Often, the rest of the work naturally begins to improve once the environment is better.

A valuable lesson I learned from the Amish and Mennonite communities comes into play at this point: their ability to build a barn in a day. It has become one of the most significant insights in my turnaround experience, particularly when it comes to the first action taken towards implementing employee recommendations. Many recommendations are directly accomplished with the cleanup. Complaints about the shop-floor bathrooms are easily remedied when you rebuild them and bring them to the same level as the executive bathrooms.

TRANSFORM YOUR WORKSPACE IN A WEEKEND

I suggest dedicating one day to planning the overhaul with your leadership team, and then three ten-hour days—Friday, Saturday, and Sunday—to doing the work with all your employees. For the extra hours and weekend days, it is best to pay everyone the same rate. This rate should be above the normal overtime rate. No matter the number of employees, this can easily mean thousands of hours dedicated to cleaning up the company to set it on a new course. The cost is an investment that pays huge dividends.

A great example of what can be accomplished with this approach, and its impact, was the turnaround acquisition I did in Scotland. The company was absolutely on its last legs with an owner who was about to lose his house due to a personal liability and a bank default. The purchase was quickly arranged, but the turnaround also had to happen very quickly in order to save the company. To add a little more color to the background, that area of Scotland had an unemployment rate of over 20% and unemployment benefits were derisibly small, so losing your job would cause devastation to your family. The general manager ruled the company with an iron hand and the sensitivity of a concentration camp guard. He terrified the employees with constant threats of being laid off. He was obviously a cancer that needed to be removed if the company had any chance of being successful. This company was in such bad shape, with financial ruin staring downtrodden employees in the face.

Counterintuitively, however, this prospect made me feel very optimistic. There was almost nothing I could do to make the company worse and a lot I could do to not only make it better but also potentially make it thrive. We had a list compiled by the employees of the action items they would like implemented, so now was the time to act.

Soon after the acquisition and company meetings, I called another company meeting to announce we would be shutting down the company on the next Thursday to create a plan for the weekend, which would entail three ten-hour days on Friday, Saturday, and Sunday. Doing the math: 3 days times 10 hours times 100 people meant 3,000 man and women hours. In order to make sure everyone benefited, we paid all the employees the maximum shop-floor pay rate for overtime. On the Sunday night we would have a catered dinner on the factory floor and an open house for family and friends so the employees could share with them what had been accomplished. Taxis would be provided to and from the factory to allow the employees to celebrate in the time-honored Scottish way, drinking copious amounts of Scotch.

One of the things I had drastically underestimated was the significant skill sets that the employees had. As we planned for the complete refurbishment of the plant, I found we had every trade imaginable represented by the employees. We had excellent carpenters, electricians, plumbers, and mechanics. There was no task for which we did not have craftsmen.

The plan of action was finalized by the end of Thursday. There was a genuine air of excitement for what we were about to undertake. Everything was planned, staged, and the renovation began. The progress was slow on the first day because there was a significant amount of material that needed to be removed. But just removing junk, unused fixtures, and unneeded tools made a big improvement. Suddenly we had more room and remnants of the past were rapidly gone. The second day, we made major progress repainting the floors and the walls, refurbishing the bathrooms, and putting skylights in the roof for natural light. Bathrooms are always a great indicator of respect for employees. Allowing them to deteriorate sends a very clear message to employees that management does not care about their well-being. Keeping every area spotless, especially bathrooms, is a great morale booster. Bathrooms for the shop floor need to be the same quality as the executive bathrooms.

I offered a glimpse of this story in an earlier chapter. As I mentioned, we did not have a union but we did have a works committee and their main job was to find the most disagreeable job for me and a pair of extra-large overalls. They assigned me to clean out a six-foot-deep pit that had accumulated steel stampings and garbage over many years. This was a fetid swamp but I wanted to show I was up to the task and would complete it as well as I could. Cleaning that pit took me almost the entire three days. It involved removing thousands of pounds of scrap metal by hand. I think all the employees were surprised by my stamina, which I hoped would give them some optimism about the company's future.

Cosmetics are also a sign of employee respect, so we installed a new sign and repainted the outside of the building. We even added flowers in the flower beds to remind employees every day as they walked in that there had been a fundamental change in the company.

Like Cortés, the Spanish explorer, we were not going back. The party on Sunday was a great success even though I had difficulty understanding the local Scottish brogue, which became more indecipherable as whiskey consumption increased.

On the Monday morning there was a new sense of pride in the company and optimism for the future. A fun anecdote I'll never forget: one of our major customers, Hewlett-Packard, had planned a visit that morning. From my office I had a view of the road that led up to our company. Here were our visitors heading towards our driveway when all of a sudden, they drove straight by. I immediately realized what had happened. They did not recognize the new building and had driven right past. They eventually did a U-turn and returned, stunned by the new paint, flowers in the flower beds, and a brand-new company that had been resurrected over a weekend. Not quite a barn built in a day, but close.

The purpose of the story is to show the hidden potential in most employees, what can be accomplished if everyone works for a common purpose. It also shows the pride of ownership that can be created with a thorough cleanup. One of the employees was a great photographer so I asked him to photograph the before and after so we could all remember what the company looked like before the cleanup.

FURTHER THOUGHTS ON TRANSFORMING THE WORKPLACE

Thirty years on, the overhaul process I've described has been refined in other companies I have worked with, including a recent company in Yakima, Washington. The same principles still applied and the results were equally spectacular. And I feel the same exhilaration today as I did in Scotland.

It is not always possible to complete the renovation in a weekend. An alternate way that is equally effective is to divide the company layout into ten grids. Identify a leader for each grid and ask them to come up with a plan, including a timeline, that will transform the area cosmetically and also improve the overall work conditions for the employees. The first task is to discard anything that is not needed. Open all the drawers and hiding places and get rid of everything you can.

You will be amazed at how many items are kept "just in case." As the grid leaders' plans unfold, transformation starts across the entire workplace.

Another good idea is sometimes to rent an external storage area for items that you are not sure if you'll use again. This can free up a lot of area within the company workspace.

WHATEVER YOUR LIST of employee recommendations may look like, don't underestimate the power of building a barn in a day. I have rarely seen quality products come from a disorganized and untidy facility. Quality starts with appearance, so make that the focus of your first action. By leveraging the resulting newfound energy and momentum of your team, you can breathe new life into the company very quickly. And that sets the tone and direction for all the improvements that are yet to come.

STEP 6

BUSINESS ASSESSMENT

The business assessment is another challenging area to address. It requires a brutal investigation into the actual business, and there are three sides to the assessment: your **customer side**, your **supplier side**, and your **employee side**.

You'll take a deeper dive into the company's relationship with customers and suppliers when you conduct stakeholder meetings in Step 7. But an initial assessment of both needs to be done. By the end of Step 6, you should have a comprehensive idea of the competitiveness of your company, what changes you need to make to improve it, and a plan to implement the employee suggestions that will directly impact suppliers and customers. This will set you up for success as you venture into your stakeholder meetings.

THE CUSTOMER SIDE

To arm yourself with valuable customer insights, start by getting more familiar with the marketplace you're selling into, and how your company fits into it. Get answers to questions such as:

- Who are your competitors?

- What do they have that you don't?

- How financially successful are they?

- Should you aim to acquire them down the line?

- Why do your customers buy from you?

- Why do they buy from your competitors?

- Do your competitors offer inducements to encourage their customers to buy from them?

Regarding this last question, yes, kickbacks are more prevalent than most people think. These inducements can be more subtle than a straight bribe and may come in the form of tickets to football games, golf trips, etc. You have to rapidly assess the landscape that you are competing in and find a way of giving your customer a superior product without resorting to bribes.

Many years ago, I bought a machining company that had two major customers. These companies were very well known in the area and could have chosen any supplier to machine parts. One of the companies made precision rifle scopes and had been around for many years. Before I bought the company, I visited this customer and the buyer assured me that they would continue doing business with us after the acquisition. He added cryptically that all the existing terms and conditions would apply to future business between us. What I naively failed to pick up on was the kickback he had been getting from my company's previous owner. We received some good follow-on orders after I bought the company, but sure enough, these started to dwindle over the next few months until they dried up completely. It was only then that I realized how the previous owner had been doing business. It was a shock to see sales drop by 50% soon after buying a business.

As this example shows, it's important in your business assessment to determine the reasons customers are buying from you. Maintaining relationships is important, but they need to be honest and genuine. Many buyers buy from a company because they like the person they are dealing with. They know that person will go to bat for them, and they know that person will provide them with a level of service that makes working with them enjoyable and effective. It is a fallacy to believe that companies always buy from the lowest-cost providers. Buyers buy mainly from people they have an honest personal relationship with and people who are enthusiastic about their company and its future. This applies to both your customers and your suppliers. Your customers buy from you and you buy from your suppliers.

THE SUPPLIER SIDE

Gathering of similar insights on the supplier side can determine how successful you will be in delivering product on behalf of all your customers. Your suppliers need to be examined very carefully. Investigate questions such as:

- Are your suppliers competitively priced?

- Have service levels deteriorated because you have not paid them on time?

- Have you beaten their prices down to a point that you get poor service, late deliveries, and poor quality?

An amusing anecdote from the past shows this situation very clearly. I was brought into a company that made plush toys for the carnival and county fair market. They were one of the largest manufacturers of plush animals in the United States. They had two major facilities, one in Chicago and the other in Los Angeles. Plush animals weigh little but factoring in maximum container volume and weight, it was impossible to have them manufactured overseas: the cost of transporting these stuffed animals would be too expensive. Instead, they imported the skins for the animals and stuffed them at their two plants. The irascible owner told his buyer that he was paying too much for the skins. Suspecting too that the buyer was getting a kickback, which he was not, the owner decided to jump on a plane to South Korea to negotiate the prices for himself. He soon returned triumphantly declaring he had reduced the price by 30%, so it seemed obvious to him that some shenanigans were taking place.

A few weeks later the containers started arriving at the plants for stuffing. Almost immediately the whole plant looked like a stuffed animal MASH unit. Arms and legs were falling off, stomachs were split from end to end, even heads were falling off. The owner had browbeaten the supplier on the price and what he ended up with was a wafer-thin skin, a single piece of thread holding on the eyes. The supplier had met the owner's price demands by reducing the quality. Eventually the hundreds of thousands of skins were replaced with a new batch at the original price, and the mangled, decapitated animals were sent to the dumpster. So be careful when you demand an unreasonably low price from suppliers; you will get what you pay for.

THE EMPLOYEE SIDE

The third leg of the triad is the employee's assessment of the company. A lot of this information is revealed through comments during the employee meetings. Do the employees feel proud of the company they work for? Do they help recruit friends? Do they tell their relatives what a great company it is to work for?

A very simple litmus test is to ask which employee has been there the longest and talk to them about why they have stayed. Valuable insight is gained by asking a prospective company how many W-2 forms they issued in the last year. This should be easy to obtain from the payroll department. One company I worked with that had been recently acquired had a little over 100 employees and over 520 W-2s. This should have been a major red flag during due diligence, but it is rare that acquirers ask for this important information. Besides the enormous cost of hiring and firing that number of people, such rapid turnover means major cost in training new employees, which takes away the productivity of the employees doing the training.

STEP 7

STAKEHOLDER MEETINGS

Stakeholder meetings are another big milestone, as they're the first time you'll acknowledge the company's financial troubles to anyone outside the company. Your four big stakeholders to address are **banks**, **investors**, **suppliers**, and **customers**. In each case, you're going to come clean about the challenges you face in working with the stakeholder— whether it's difficulty paying off a bank's loan or a customer contract that is causing you to lose money. What is needed is a win-win solution for all involved.

Your goal across the board is to figure out how to continue doing *profitable* business with each stakeholder. In most cases cash has dried up, or it's about to dry up, and your current arrangement with them no longer works. Perhaps your company has faced financial distress before and found a way around the problems. Often, such solutions involve kicking the can down the road. For example, one very tempting quick source of cash is to tap into the quarterly taxes that have been deducted from employees but not yet remitted to the IRS and state tax departments. I see this happen often. Don't do it. It's not worth it. Chances are, if the situation is that bad, you won't have the money to cover the remittance when it's due. The interest from the IRS starts ten days after you receive notice of a missed payment and can go as high as 15%. Then there is the interest penalty from state tax authorities. This is one of the most expensive loans you can find and could result in additional payments and personal liabilities. I have had to intercede a couple of times with the IRS to resolve nonpayment of 941 obligations, in one case even pledging tax refunds to take care of the nonpayment.

"Solutions" like these cover up and perpetuate the problem—and they're not necessary. You can find a win-win solution to nearly any stakeholder issue if you're forthright about your troubles and come prepared with a reasonable path forward.

BANK AND INVESTOR MEETINGS

These are the most difficult and tense meetings. Investors and banks always expect the worst. The first rule is complete honesty. You must explain how bad things are, but it is just as important to assure these stakeholders that you have found all the bodies that have been buried. You have one chance to establish credibility so you cannot blow it. Full disclosure means no damaging revelations later on that could undermine your credibility. There needs to be a detailed explanation of the current situation, warts and all, and how and why it happened. The more thorough and accurate the explanation, the more reassuring it will be to them. In some cases, it will not be as bad as they thought.

Don't ever gloss over how bad things are. This is the last chance to gain their support; understating the depth of the problem sets you up for failure. However, describing the reality of the current low point gives you a great opportunity to then outline the detailed plan for recovery, including steps that have already been started. This goes a long way in establishing your credibility that there is light at the end of the tunnel rather than an oncoming train. Your level of honesty may mark the first time in many years that they feel confidence in the company.

With banks, in particular, it is good to point out that this is the worst the company will ever get. Even if they did not know how bad things were, they will be relieved to finally have the truth, everything out in the open. The drip-drip-drip of disclosures is the worst scenario for a bank and frequently causes them to act irrationally out of fear. You can normally eliminate the chance of the bank overreacting with full disclosure.

Empty the Accounting Closet

This is the time to throw caution to the wind and lay out all the items that have no real market value but have been held on the books (for who knows how long!). Inevitably, this will cause bank covenant breaches, but these were probably breached a long time ago if more realistic financial reporting had occurred. Many companies, aided and abetted by their financial team, have repeatedly kicked the can down the road. Eventually, there is no can left to kick.

There are some situations that need to be handled with extreme caution, where a company has fraudulently misrepresented assets. This mainly happens in inventory valuations but can also happen in misrepresenting accounts receivables. Banks normally have a formula to calculate how much you can borrow against accounts receivables. Each month you send in a borrowing certificate that calculates how much you can borrow. The most common formula is 50% of inventory and 80% of eligible receivables. Inventory percentage can vary depending on the type of inventory, whether it is raw materials, work in progress, or finished goods.

Accounts receivables borrowing is normally limited to 80% of your accounts receivable that are less than 90 days past due. This is where the squeeze play starts. When you are funding losses through bank lines of credit, the funding train eventually grinds to a halt. It also encourages companies to less aggressively collect receivables because they can get an advance of 80% immediately from the bank. This means that when the payment is eventually received, 80% goes to the bank and the company is left with 20%. This works when sales are growing because the borrowing base is always increasing.

The rub comes when sales decrease, and all the cash from receivables goes to paying down the bank. Now you have a real dilemma because you still haven't addressed the fact that the company is losing money and you have completely run out of cash. This is when companies frequently resort to mispresenting assets to the bank—probably the politest phrase for what it is: fraud. You have fraudulently mispresented your assets to borrow money. This can be a felony in most states.

Full disclosure is often the best way to head this off at the pass, together with an aggressive process of remediation and commitment to financially address the deficit that has been covered up by the fraud. The bank basically wants its money back. As Mark Twain so elegantly put it, "I am more concerned with the return of my money than the return of my money."

I had a client recently who had been systematically overvaluing their inventory. The owner of the company completely denied it even after I walked through the warehouse where the inventory was stored and did the dust test. Running your hand over the inventory to see if it's covered in dust is a very easy way to determine whether it has any market value. If there is dust, it hasn't moved! Valuable inventory does not collect dust.

The bank in this case was also negligent. They had not visited the company's warehouse and relied on collateral reports that the financial director had put together. The owner claimed to have no knowledge of the inventory fraud. The CFO, on the other hand, said the owner had made him put the false numbers together. "I didn't know" does not really work as a defense. The infamous *ignorantia juris neminem excusat* (ignorance of the law is no excuse) is the legal pillar that eliminates this defense.

So, what should a company in such a position do? First, get all the facts together. Make sure they are accurate and up-to-date. Put together a plan to remedy the overborrowing as soon as possible and share it with the bank.

Moving Forward Together

Both investors and bankers are always relieved when they see a realistic recovery plan with some major changes already implemented. They don't want to get in the way of a good thing. Any significant layoffs need to have taken place before the bank meeting. Offering to significantly reduce officers' and senior executives' pay also goes a long way to improve the relationship with both banks and investors.

Make sure all the stakeholders feel the recovery is inevitable and already underway. One by-product of recognizing the significant operating losses is a restatement of previously published financial statements. This offers a light at the end of the tunnel because the company has been paying taxes on profits they were not making. The restatement of your financial statements invariably results in a significant tax rebate. Normally loss carrybacks are limited to three years from the date you filed. In most cases, I chose to do this before the bank meetings. This allowed me to tell the bank there would be an infusion of cash in the near future from the tax rebate. Sometimes the amounts were very large (hundreds of thousands of dollars). In many cases, this cash was the new capital the company needed and further turbocharged the recovery.

The most important thing is that the root cause of all the problems described above was not recognizing operating losses when they were occurring. Denial is a very strong instinct when facing danger. Running away from the fire does not put it out; denying that it exists makes the conflagration worse. Being afraid of your bank or investors and avoiding confrontation only makes matters worse. In forty years of working with banks, I have found that they have all acted rationally, even when faced with situations of outright fraud. They want to resolve the issues with the company as much as you do. A viable company that they have lent money to is their lifeline. You just have to show them the way.

SUPPLIER MEETINGS

Contact your suppliers and customers soon after your meetings with the banks and investors. I prefer to meet with suppliers before customers to make sure I have their support to meet the customers' expectations. Without having reliable suppliers on its side, it's impossible for a company to meet its customers' requirements. Suppliers are a company's lifeblood and need to be taken care of if the company wants to survive.

Suppliers are in a similar position as the bank except with little or no security. They want to continue shipping, but at some point, they do not want to add any more risk. The most obvious warning that a supplier is becoming weary, and wary, of you is when they change your payment terms from 30–60 days to COD (cash on delivery). Frequently, this is the final straw before a company collapses. The cash drain caused by COD payments precipitates other bills not being paid and companies go into a death spiral.

You are aiming to achieve two things when you approach key suppliers, particularly if they are sole-source suppliers. You want to, first, give them complete confidence that they are going to be paid for all future shipments and, second, ensure that they are not going to change your terms to COD.

Before reaching out to suppliers, get clear on exactly what you owe to each one. You should already have this information from your Step 2 audit of accounts payables. It is a good idea to ring-fence what is already owed and then discuss with them your future purchasing requirements. At this point, to give them confidence in a future business relationship, let them know the remedial financial steps that you have already put in place.

When you have fully confirmed the amount owed, it is a good time to introduce the idea of providing them a note payable with interest for the current debt. This can have two major benefits: one, they can get interest on their outstanding payables, and two, they won't have to write the amount off.

The final persuasion sometimes has to include a personal guarantee, so a quick word about those. Personal guarantees are frequently required by banks where there is single or family ownership. The bank wants to make sure everyone has a stake in the outcome of the business and can't just walk away and leave the bank holding the defunct company. However, there are no limits to the number of personal guarantees that a person can have outstanding, so they can way exceed their entire assets. There is also no priority to the claim. The first one to the courthouse wins. Not that I would encourage offering unlimited personal guarantees, but if giving one encourages a supplier to keep on shipping, then as part of the turnaround it may be worth it. Creating long-term debt out of current liabilities helps the balance sheet of a company by improving the current ratio.

A Creditor Committee for All

Many years ago, I was presented with a completely insolvent company that had twice as many current liabilities as current assets (current ratio). This meant that what the company owed in the next twelve months would have them paying out twice as much money as they had coming in. This is the classic definition of insolvency.

There was only one option for me as the consultant responsible for turning the company around, and that was to broker a deal with their suppliers. To do this, I created a sort of creditor committee of suppliers. This approach allows you to deal with the suppliers collectively as a group rather than negotiate with them individually. The recommendation here is to treat everyone the same, with exactly the same terms and conditions. No preferential treatment regardless of size, obligation amount, or how long overdue. The option I presented to them at least gave them some chance of getting their debts paid. Important to add, as part of my negotiation, turning current payables into a note also required the supplier to continue shipping product on their normal terms. As well, the company made the commitment to honor these terms, including payment on the note.

The advantage to the supplier is that even if the company only survived for a year, some of the debt would be paid down. If suppliers refused the offer of debt consolidation and a note payable then they would lose everything in a bankruptcy.

I had an early introduction to this sort of arrangement when I was twenty-seven years old and working my way through my second turnaround. Maybe it was my youthful bravado and feeling that I had nothing to lose that gave me the confidence to set off and meet with the CFO of a very large multi-billion-dollar company to discuss how to take care of a $7 million payable. It was certainly do or die, because if I could not come to an agreement with them, all bets were off.

The company we owed so much money to was Seagram, with an office at 375 Park Avenue in New York City. Seagram was kind enough to put me up in a suite at The Pierre in

Manhattan near Central Park. It was a wonderful place with all the old-world charm of a hotel that opened in 1930. A note at the front desk informed me that a car would pick me up at nine o'clock the following morning to take me to the headquarters at 375 Park Avenue, a short ride away.

Soon I was standing in the spacious office of the chairman and CEO of Seagram, Edgar Bronfman Jr., who was a very imposing man but had a kind smile. I think he was somewhat bemused by his young visitor from Seattle. He asked what he could do for me, and without any hesitation, I explained the difficult financial situation that my client was in and that there were very limited options on how it could be resolved. The only option I could offer was for Seagram to take the debt and turn it into a long-term note with interest. If I could persuade him to accept my offer, the company would cease to be insolvent. Although it would still have a significant debt load, this debt could be paid down when the company was profitable. While this would not solve their financial problems, it would give the company some breathing room and keep the suppliers shipping product to them.

Mr. Bronfman was a little taken aback by my proposal and then paused and asked if I would mind if he brought in his CFO to review my offer. When the CFO joined us, I explained that the bank had first lien on all the company inventory so Seagram, as a totally unsecured creditor, would probably receive nothing if the company went bankrupt. "Quite an offer," he said. "If we don't agree, we will have to write off seven million dollars." I told him that my proposal was the only way I could see him getting paid in full. I let him know I would further enhance the offer by offering to accelerate the pay down of the note with profits that I intended to make soon when the company was turned around.

He was very skeptical and pointed out how unlikely this was since the company had not been very profitable for many years. Suddenly he changed the subject and said, "I hope you are going to offer the same deal to all the suppliers you owe money to." I assured him all suppliers were going to get the same offer and I was planning to visit a number of other companies on this trip. With a smile, he said, "I know who all your suppliers are and they are good friends of mine. Would you mind if I gave them a call and told them about the deal we have put together?" I said I would greatly appreciate it. I then shook his hand, turned around, and left his office with an extraordinary feeling of exhilaration for having effectively created a creditors committee of suppliers that had agreed to convert substantial current debt into a long-term note.

CUSTOMER MEETINGS

The Seagram anecdote illustrates a number of points, the first being that sometimes you have to be fearless in dealing with suppliers or customers. Many years ago, a friend who knew I had just started my career in turnarounds gave me a small plaque with this question on it: "Can they hang you?" The answer is always, "no." Referring to the plaque gave me the courage to confront some very difficult situations. You need to give yourself permission to take the risk of confronting both suppliers and customers with an honest appraisal of the current situation. They both hold your future in their hands.

When it comes to the last stakeholder group, your customers, we have been taught that they are always right. Unfortunately, this is not always the case. A sales contract with a customer that is priced too competitively needs to be changed or terminated. I had a recent case where the only way for a company to achieve profitability was to cancel a number of sales contracts. Even a significant loss of sales was better than continuing to ship at a loss.

I vividly remember a similar situation with a customer of one of my manufacturing companies that represented close to 70% of our business. We manufactured over five hundred different parts for them and were at the receiving end of a very dysfunctional purchase order system. They were ordering components they didn't need and not ordering components they did need—this created chaos in our manufacturing system, and timely delivery went out the window. MRP systems rely on an accurate counting of inventory. If this is not done correctly, you end up with the ordering nightmare described above. This customer had a very erratic inventory counting system. These erroneous amounts fed into their material planning system. This caused chaotic ordering on their part, with damaging impact on us. There was only one resolution to this problem: I would purchase all the customer's inventory of our components so they would not have to count the inventory in stock. I then shipped product in four kits rather than five hundred individual parts. We could also determine exactly how many aircraft of a particular type they needed to build. This would allow us to smoothly manufacture directly to their demand.

On our end, this resolution was simple. The challenge was in confronting our biggest customer and convincing them to completely change their purchasing system. The current system was killing us because we could not plan effective production for the shop floor. They would order parts they did not need and were constantly making purchase order changes. This start/stop process is a nightmare for a manufacturing company because you need to have predictable and smooth production flow on the shop floor. We had to change if we were going to survive, so I decided confronting our major customer and strongly requesting a change was a risk worth taking.

To my surprise, they fully agreed. We became the first supplier that delivered product on a daily basis, matching exactly with their factory's production requirements. Problem solved!

One-on-One Proposals

It can be worth taking a risk and presenting an entirely new arrangement with a customer, especially if your current contract with them is onerous. Sometimes it's even worthwhile to throw down the gauntlet with the customer and potentially lose their business. Although I have never had a situation where a customer arbitrarily canceled their business, except where a kickback was involved.

It is difficult for a company to change suppliers, and doing so carries a significant risk that the new supplier might be worse than the incumbent. This gives even a small supplier some leverage with their customers. You cannot take advantage of your customers but there is less inequality than you might think. This is particularly true in the aerospace business because of the cost and complications of qualifying a new supplier. There have been many incidents where suppliers have been replaced and the new supplier has caused so many problems that the original equipment manufacturer (OEM) had to come back, cap in hand, to the original supplier.

Customer-supplier relationships are a two-way street. Don't be afraid to let your customer know if their actions, or your arrangement, negatively impacts your business. You need to recommend to them the steps they need to implement to improve the relationship. If suppliers are treated badly by their customers, they will eventually vote with their feet. For example, a common issue among suppliers and customers is payment terms. Prior to COVID, payment terms from some OEMs were 30 days after shipment. Post-COVID, many have now moved to 60, 90, or even 120 days after shipment and invoice. This is untenable, and at some point, you have to decide whether it is financially feasible to continue business with a customer that stretches out payment terms that way. Normally that would indicate a company's own financial stress, so it might be a good time to decide whether you want to risk doing business with them anymore, as you might not get paid at all.

STEP 8

QUALITY AND PROCESS IMPROVEMENT

Much of your turnaround work so far has focused on building your team and uncovering the problems that got your company into financial trouble. Now in Step 8, you'll focus on improving the processes behind every employee's job. Along the way, you'll also improve the quality of everyone's work.

Quality can be a very strong differentiator between companies. A company that has financial challenges frequently has quality issues as well. As their quality deteriorates, their customers desert them, creating more downward financial pressure on the company ... and it all becomes a death spiral that seals their eventual fate.

As you focus on improving quality and processes, you'll see that some of your efforts build on work you initiated in earlier steps. Personnel assessments continue here, for example, since improving processes includes figuring out what employees do all day so you can optimize their work. By this point you'll have a strong sense of what your employees do, but analyzing processes often brings even more truths to light.

If you made radical improvements to the cosmetics of the company, that's another major step towards introducing a new vision of quality. You've also met with suppliers and customers, discussed any supplier shortcomings, and been informed of any quality concerns among your customers. This chapter builds on that work so you can take quality and process improvement to the next level.

Before we dig into those strategies, there's still a lot you can accomplish with some basic changes.

START WITH THE SIMPLE

Quality begins with a person's first interaction with the company, whether through its website or by phone. It is worth making a significant investment in your company website when funds are available. A new website always gives the impression of a new beginning. The person who visits the website needs to be able to obtain relevant information quickly and easily and be informed enough to act. Reviewing the website's search engine optimization (SEO) can also benefit the turnaround. Working with an expert to optimize your SEO can elevate your website's ranking in a keyword search. I know firsthand with one of my own companies how an investment in this area can dramatically increase the number and quality of inquiries that a company receives.

Another obvious but often overlooked area for quality improvement is how the phones are answered. Even with the use of cell phones, the message that the caller gets when the recipient is unavailable needs to be coherent and upbeat rather than a robotic repeat of the cell number. Potential customers still contact companies directly and the experience of how they are treated goes a long way in their decision to give a company their business. The person who answers the phone needs to be genuinely upbeat. They need to feel that every call is a customer about to place a major order—not that every call will be, but it is certainly a possibility. The person answering the phone and manning the reception is normally seen as low person on the totem pole. This is one of the most important positions in the company. Yet how rarely is it treated that way. The person who holds this job determines how people view the overall quality of the company. If the person is knowledgeable, i.e., knows everyone in the company and knows the products really well, and enjoys their job, a first-time caller's impression of the company changes radically.

And finally, before you start strategizing process improvements, pay attention to cosmetics and the overall work environment if you haven't done so already. Nothing indicates more effectively that a company is changing than a dramatic change of appearance. A new coat of paint can transform an area and have everyone feeling that something positive is happening. In a recent engagement, the CEO was exhausted and needed something to indicate that he was starting afresh. Space on a mezzanine level above the factory—right outside his office—was the company dumping ground. Old copiers and files were scattered everywhere. It truly reflected how the employees viewed themselves and the company. All the employees' desks were piled with papers. It was obvious that however hard the employees worked, they were impeded daily by a complete lack of organization and overall cleanliness. Cleaning everything up is very inexpensive and quick. Even a complete company refurbishment is nowhere near as expensive as maintaining an inefficient, depressed, and disorganized status quo. The return on investment can be in months rather than years and that does not include the psychological benefits of working in a pleasant environment.

We had to start somewhere if this manufacturing company was going to move in the right direction. What better place than right outside the CEO's office? I asked the CEO to come in over the weekend, unannounced, to make the area spotless, and to include his own office in the cleanup. I also recommended he replace his desk with a conference table and invest in modern telecommunications equipment so that the image of his company would be modern and technologically advanced when he held remote meetings. It is stunning how many companies, even very large ones that I visit, still have computer and presentation equipment that is over twenty years old. The first part of any meeting is always a mad scramble to find the connections to laptops and presentations that are compatible with everyone's equipment and software. This can easily be simplified and standardized. There are many inexpensive Bluetooth options that can eliminate all the cables, mess, and confusion.

On the Monday morning after the CEO had transformed his office and the area outside his office, a new day had started.

Modern technology and paperless, organized workspaces are essential across any company. In fact, as you start exploring new ways to improve, you'll find that evaluating and upgrading technology, and simply getting organized, are at the heart of most quality and process improvements. Along the way you'll need to discuss what exactly quality is to your company and what levels of quality can be achieved or are practical. But you can't get far until you first figure out what's holding you back.

GET TO THE ROOT CAUSE

Where do you start with quality and process improvement? Luckily there is a very simple method to determine which changes will have the biggest impact. The starting point is a humble pareto chart broken down into three sections: Suppliers, Customers, and Internal. In each area a chart is created to analyze root causes of any defects.

The root cause analysis is the fastest way to not only start making quality improvements but also get to the real reason why there are quality problems at all. When highlighted, these problems force you to find out why it is happening. For example, when I introduced the requirement to record all measurements taken on the shop floor at my aerospace manufacturing company QPM, what happened was a big surprise.

First, measuring anything accurately is of value, but when making flight-critical aerospace components, you have to have accurate measurements to make sure they stay within a very tight tolerance. And if they are out of tolerance, you need to know the reason so it does not happen again. This is called root cause analysis. Finding the root cause involves detective work so it is valuable to start this process as quickly as possible while the trail is still warm. A cold case is a lot more difficult. Once the root cause has been determined, you need to implement a corrective action. If the root cause is correctly identified and the corrective action implemented, then the issue should not occur again, resulting in a quality improvement.

The rollout of the root cause analysis at QPM involved the new quality management software I had developed called Net-Inspect. The software maintains every specification for a part being made. When a machinist measured a part and the result was outside the specification, they were required to identify the reason it was out of tolerance from a drop-down list of groups of root causes. This allowed us to quickly figure out which item had caused the problem. It also allowed us to group together similar root causes where one corrective action would solve many problems. The surprise came at day's end when my quality control manager came to me and said the system is a disaster: there had been over two hundred out-of-tolerance measurements in the first day that the system was used. He was a little taken aback when I told him that was great. Then when I asked him what the number one cause was, he said machining offset errors. Offsets are a way an operator makes minor changes to the machining process by entering a complex set of numbers directly into the CNC (computerized numerical control), a fancy name for a machine tool whose path is controlled by a computer. When the numerical offsets are entered, it is very easy to make a typo. A one-digit error can sometimes crash the machine, although the most benign outcome is that the part being machined is out of tolerance. We found out through the pareto chart that the number one cause for out of tolerance components was, by far, offset errors. More than half of our defects were directly related to this cause. We held a quick meeting to determine how we could eliminate this root cause. With a resigned look on his face, my plant manager said if you really want to get rid of offsets, then you need to network all the machines and purchase a laser presetter.

I asked him why we hadn't done this before. He replied that it was very expensive. What he eventually realized was that the scrap and rework we were creating every day would have paid for the system in less than three months.

The main lesson from this exercise was that collecting accurate data and charting allowed the company to make massive quality improvements very quickly. We made a

50% improvement by taking the single action of purchasing a laser presetter.

In a manufacturing company, quality improvement is a critical part of the turnaround, together with creating a zero-defect environment. As a postscript, this process allowed my company to be a genuine zero-defect manufacturing facility, making it one of the most profitable companies I have owned. (There is probably another book in the wings, *The 10-Day Plan to Eliminate Defects*, but that's for another day.)

The main takeaway here is that dramatic quality improvements change a company for the better, both financially and organizationally. Elimination of escapements improves your reputation with your customers. Elimination of defects internally decreases costs and increases profits for your company. Eliminating defects in your suppliers avoids latent defects contaminating your products.

A complete quality transformation takes time. It begins with changing the company's philosophy about quality so you can start moving in a new direction. The complete process will take a number of months but will be one of the most productive processes, particularly in a manufacturing environment. In the next section, which also ties into quality, I describe areas in companies that I call the departments of corrections. This applies to all types of companies, not just manufacturing.

Quality improvements and high-quality expectations bring new pride to the employees and help create a new vision for the company going forward.

ELIMINATE THE DEPARTMENT OF CORRECTIONS

One of the things that always concerned me when I analyzed a company was how many people's jobs were dedicated to correcting what other people had not done properly in the first place. Early on I christened these the "departments of corrections." They occur in all types of companies and tie into their quality.

I found the ultimate department of corrections in a large manufacturing company that I was brought in to help. This company had twenty relatively autonomous divisions that provided regional manufacturing for the products that the company produced. Squirreled away in the large accounting department were four employees whose desks were piled with papers. Every time I walked by this department, I heard audible groans as they looked at a new batch of work they had to complete. This department ran up a considerable amount of overtime to make sure all was done before the accounting books closed at the end of each month.

I decided I was going to get to the bottom of what caused these employees to look and sound so depressed. My first task was to find out exactly what they did and why it was so tortuous. I sat down next to one of the employees, and she immediately went into a long description of the challenges the department had. This department had two functions: one was to enter all the divisional payroll data and the other was to pay the bills for all divisions. The volumes were quite large but that was not the problem. Their main challenge was not entering the data but correcting it. The invoices frequently had the wrong general ledger number on them for distribution on the chart of accounts. To add to their workload, when completing the payroll, the numbers were frequently incorrect and had to be reconfirmed with the divisions.

With no forewarning, I posed this question to everyone: "What would happen if everything that came in from the divisions was correct?" The reaction was uniformly immediate and vocal. "We would not have anything to do. Ninety percent of our daily work is correcting other people's mistakes." This was perceived as a tiresome but virtuous task because without their intervention employees would not be paid correctly and invoices would not be paid and distributed correctly.

The remedy was obvious to me. I sent a notice to all the branch managers that from that day forward, if the payroll data was incorrect, it would not be paid. It would be sent back to the branch and the branch managers would have to resubmit the data accurately. The same principle would be applied to the invoices: if they were not correct, they would not be paid. This would leave the division managers in the unenviable position of having angry employees and suppliers who hadn't been paid storming their office. The vision of angry employees and vendors pounding at their door caused the managers to make sure all information sent to the corporate office was correct. This eliminated the need for a non-value-added department.

These gradual changes are different from the first very abrupt reduction in force that was needed to save the ship. If you recall, at that point employees would have been told that there would be no further reductions on this scale, although changes would be brought on by efficiency and better use of technology. What I've described above is one of those circumstances.

Search Out the Safety Nets

Step 4, Personnel Assessment, is a good time to find departments of corrections. Most exist as safety nets. You need to ask yourself what the root cause of the need for correction is and implement action that targets where the error occurs. Unfortunately, the safety net gets imbedded into the workflow, and like many things during a turnaround, no one knows how to get rid of them. The simple way is to identify root causes. When the real root cause of a problem is identified and corrected, there is little or no need for a safety net. The lack of a safety net also makes employees more careful if they know no one is going to correct their errors.

It is always difficult to persuade employees that they do not need a safety net. The response is always: "What would happen if ..." This is where competence and confidence are required, it also comes from training and high expectations of employees to do everything correctly all the time.

Making sure everyone understands the downstream effects and costs of their mistakes is also important. Creating foolproof methods and procedures to eliminate errors is a long-term, permanent fix. Technology plays a large part in this, which is highlighted in more detail below in discussion of automation, technology, and the elimination of a paper.

Analyze Every Job

The only way to really root out departments of corrections is to scrutinize every job. Every job should identify exactly what the person does and the procedures they have to follow. The ISO 9000, which is similar to the aerospace version, AS9100, is a defined quality process. Part of becoming ISO or AS certified is to identify who is responsible for every task and what the procedure is for every task. All of this is documented. Companies are then audited by a third party who stops and asks an employee at random what they are doing. They then ask the employee where the procedure for what they are doing is written down. This is to make sure all employees follow a specific procedure for a specific task. The quality manual is a written set of procedures that ensures the same process is followed for a task every time. This is a good place to start when trying to identify departments of corrections. When you workflow a person's job and part of their job is to correct or check processes that should have previously been done correctly, the departments of corrections become very obvious.

A person's job needs to add value. Checking someone else's work subtracts rather than adds value. Equally tragic is when a person's skills and talents are underutilized because they are wasting everyone's time checking for errors. This was the case in a new factory I built in Portland, Oregon, that manufactured precision aerospace components. In many cases these components had very tight tolerances so quality of manufacturing was key to the success of the company. The company grew very quickly from $1 million in revenue to over $30 million in the first ten years. But alarmingly, one of the departments that was growing the fastest was my inspection department. I was told to expect this because the volume and complexity of the parts we were manufacturing needed careful inspection to make sure they were manufactured correctly.

It was then that the light bulb went on. What would happen if we made the components so accurately that, statistically, there were no defects? Would we need to inspect the parts to make sure they were correct when we could guarantee that statistically the defect rate on the features was 3.4 defects per million (Six Sigma) parts produced? Aerospace production traditionally has very low production rates, with the two major companies, Airbus and Boeing, manufacturing only thirty to fifty aircrafts per month, with many having only two of our components per aircraft. This means that in most cases we would need to manufacture only one hundred components each month. If we maintained the Six Sigma rate of 3.4 defects per million parts, a defect would occur approximately once every forty-one years. It probably would not be worth having an entire department looking for something that would occur so infrequently. Without getting too much into the weeds with statistical process control, this example illustrates the danger of making assumptions that the traditional way should always be repeated.

In this case, the company was able to reduce its inspection department from fourteen people to two with a very valuable reassignment of a number of employees. I'd mentioned in Step 4 that many of the inspectors at this company were seasoned machinists who only became inspectors because it paid more. Their true love was machining. They really enjoyed mentoring younger employees and here they were trapped in work they disliked and prevented from doing the work they enjoyed because it paid less. Because of an arbitrary pay decision, we had created a perverse incentive for some very talented employees: get paid more and end up doing work you don't enjoy. This happens frequently when talented employees get promoted into management when they would happily stay in their current jobs if it paid the same as a manager. For this situation, the remedy was obvious: the inspectors who used to be machinists went back to being machinists at an inspector's pay rate. The two people who did not have a machinist background became roving inspectors. They spent their time auditing measuring techniques used by the machine operators to check that their manufactured parts were conforming. They also reviewed the operator's capability to maintain the process control required to eliminate the need for traditional inspection.

Check that It's Right

Yes, it's important to check that everything is done as it's supposed to, but this shouldn't require an entire department. Checklists are one helpful tool to make sure everything is done correctly. There is a general perception that checklists are a waste of time. I disagree. One example of their validity is in the cockpit of an airplane: this checklist procedure followed on every flight. A dramatic example of a failure to follow a checklist played out on a Gulfstream jet, which had a locking device on the elevator to restrict its movement in high winds when the aircraft is parked. The crew of this particular jet failed to verify, as part of the standard checklist, that the locking device had been disengaged and proceeded to try to take off, with catastrophic results. Everyone lost their life, an $80-million plane was destroyed, and the reputation of Gulfstream took a major hit when their flagship aircraft crashed.

WHETHER YOU CHOOSE a defined process or a checklist to make sure work is completed correctly, you will be able to quarantine defects in place and limit the damage they can make downline. The primary task is to uncover the root cause that created a need for a department of corrections.

ASSESS YOUR AUTOMATION AND TECHNOLOGY

As you begin to uncover root causes and streamline workflow, it's a great time to also evaluate the company's automation and technology. Start by assessing the current level of technology. There are many cases where the existing technology is just not being used. A great example of this was with one of my manufacturing companies that had very advanced machine tools. When these tools were purchased, I was concerned whether we would use all the technology available on them. For full disclosure, I have absolutely no mechanical skills at all.

Even with this lack of competence, I decided to undertake a little experiment. I wanted to see if we were using all the technology that came with the machine tool. I selected a large CNC machine cell and went down to the plant in Portland, Oregon. I asked the operator if he would like the day off with pay. He seemed genuinely alarmed when I told him I was going to operate his machine for the day. It was common knowledge that I didn't have a machining background. He was convinced that you needed at least five years' experience to operate equipment as sophisticated as a 16-pallet two-machine cell.

I asked how long he thought it would take him to teach me how to run it and he said years. I told him he needed to teach me in an hour and he could then have the rest of the day off with pay. He then explained that if he only had an hour to teach me, then he would have to simplify the process. "If you are going to run it on your own, we are going to have to use the automatic planning system," he said. I did not know the system had an automatic scheduling system to load and unload all the materials into the machine. I asked why he didn't use it, and he said that if he did, he wouldn't have anything to do.

What a revelation that was: technology not being used because it would work too well. He then offered to set up all the pallets on the CNC so they arrived at the machining center in sequence. My only job was to load and unload the pallets and inspect the material—hardly a job that would take five years to learn. He quickly showed me how to load, unload, and inspect the parts when they were finished. After inspection, they would automatically go back to the station where the material was loaded and unloaded.

It dawned on me that, ironically, a lot of the technology in my own company where I prided myself on the utilization of advanced technology was not being used. So, when you start to evaluate a company's technology, the very first thing to look at is what you have and make sure it's being used to its maximum capability.

There are many reasons why technology is not used. In some cases, it is not universally loved. But often, it's because a certain technology is a direct threat to an individual's job and/or a capability that has been honed for many years. There is a sense of pride and an obvious reluctance to have technology replace one's capability, or even just improve upon it. Technology by definition takes traditional manual skills and evaporates them in front of everyone's eyes. The need for people's individual skills will continue to diminish significantly as technology advances and as computers and robots produce products more reliably. Reluctance to incorporate technology becomes a case of turkeys not wanting to vote for Thanksgiving. The impact and the concern become very obvious: *If I implement this technology, what will happen to my job?*

This is a very hard hurdle to overcome, and it has to be addressed in a sensitive way.

If a company is profitable and growing, you can always reassign someone to a different task, which is why staying profitable and lean is so vital to the future of the company. There is always a major pushback on technology, especially in manufacturing companies. There are so many traditional skills that have been learned that can now easily be replaced with technology. That transition is very, very difficult. The positive side is that there are fewer and fewer people who want to do the traditional jobs, and younger people coming into the workforce expect technology. Handed a piece of paper, they will look at it in horror. Many CEOs' nine-year-old daughters are way more adept at utilizing technology than their C-suite parent. The generation starting to enter the workforce arrives fully comfortable with technology. They also expect it to be available for their use on day one. If it's not, they will decline the opportunity to work for your company. Lack of technology will further exacerbate the problems that companies have in hiring and retaining good employees.

GET YOUR DATA DUCKS IN A ROW

Alongside evaluating and upgrading technology, as I mentioned earlier, simply getting organized is at the heart of most quality and process improvements. This is especially true for your data. Disorganized data has as much potential to hold a company back as any other company inefficiency. What's worse is that this problem is often overlooked since software and data can so easily be dispersed and decentralized without anyone even realizing it has happened. As you take a holistic view of your quality and processes, keep the following steps in mind to optimize the company's data practices.

Centralize Stored Data

An early action item in your technology review is to meet with the person in charge of IT and learn where the company's data is stored. Is it cloud based? Is there a central server? Or is it scattered throughout all the company's individual PCs? Are there inventories of all the PCs and the data stored on each? When all this information has been compiled, go through all the data collected and start a cleanup similar to the one that was done of the physical location.

One area that I always look at during this process is all the Excel spreadsheets that exist. These are company property and should only be kept on the company server, not on an individual's computer. It's also important to examine who is using the spreadsheets and, more importantly, why they needed this information. The data could be valuable to other people, but not when sequestered on someone's computer.

Creating your own spreadsheet, especially if it is complicated, gives an employee significant power. Some of the need for spreadsheets is due to poor responses from a corporate IT department, but mostly it's a desire to have your own information source. One of the challenges with this is that there is no way to verify whether the information is correct. I have also seen major mistakes made by financial analysts in acquisition because no one checked the math and formulas in their spreadsheets.

Streamline the Data You Keep

To build on the preceding point, it's so important to have reliable and accessible data. A few years ago, I was asked to talk to a group of senior people in Washington, DC, who were involved in the F-35 Joint Strike Fighter program. They wanted me to discuss big data and then look at their areas in relation to that. They had gigabytes of data but were not able to extract any value from it. As I planned my talk, I knew that creating an acronym would help the audience accept my recommendations. The acronym I came up with was TAPA, and I explained it like this:

- **T = timely** If data is out of date, it has no value whatsoever. It is yesterday's news. It may be of interest, but it certainly is of no real value.

- **A = accurate** It's amazing how frequently data is relied upon when no one has confirmed its accuracy or even its source. Accuracy in data is absolutely critical since wrong decisions can be made using erroneous data. And the data needs to come from a reliable source. Otherwise, the big data may have been corrupted. Then it not only has no value but also is potentially dangerous.

- **P = personalized** All big data analysis needs to be organized in a way that makes it personal to the individual who receives it. The recipient should not have to go through vast quantities of data to find what is relevant to them. Also make sure that the recipient has the data in the exact format that is useful to them.

- **A = actionable** The data needs to prompt you to take action. It shouldn't just be general reading but should cause you to do something.

All big data should be TAPA: Timely–Accurate–Personalized–Actionable. This principle needs to be applied uniformly throughout the company. It is amazing how much useless data gets stored, and how many computer reports are generated that are not used. Even worse, all that clutter makes it difficult for teams to access the data they *do* need. It's a lose-lose situation until a company puts in the work to streamline their data.

Get Rid of Paper

Part of the cleanup process includes evaluating paper and figuring out what steps can be taken to eliminate it, period. One good way to start this review is to identify every document and paper form used in every department. Then simply ask: What is the paper for? What benefit does filling it in offer? What would happen if the paper just disappeared or became an electronic document where the data on it could be accessed?

It has always shocked me how many times I have been told, "This is just the way we have always done it." No rationale of why, and no rationale to its purpose. It's just always been done this way. Well, that is never a good enough reason to continue doing anything.

Aside from the fact that it's not possible to analyze data that's stuck on paper, the cost to prepare those reports is enormous, and of little value when it's completed because no one can find the data easily. Eliminating paper provides benefits in a couple of ways. First, you can store almost unlimited data from documents either locally or in cloud storage. Second, as long as you intentionally store your information as data and not just PDF copies of documents, that data can be analyzed. This process is dramatically simplified with modern AI software. The data is where the value is, and with modern methods to analyze this data in real time, particularly in cloud technology, new insights and revelations can be gained into the operations of a company. Paper documents and PDFs of documents have very little value and cannot be collated and analyzed in the same way that data stored in the cloud can be.

When there is no alternative to paper, scan it, store it, and make it universally accessible. This is particularly a problem in the aerospace industry that I have worked in for many years. There were millions of pieces of paper that had to be kept and stored. One area that produced enormous quantities of paper was the quality department and their first articles (documents that are required prior to a new part being manufactured or if there is a change in the manufacturing process). The documentation for a new airplane has well over fifty million documents. First articles alone represent over twenty million documents. I used to joke that the airplane, once certified, would be unable to fly over the paper if it was stacked two hundred pages to the inch.

Do a Software Inventory

Finally, take stock of your software. It is frequently a big surprise to find software that has never been used sitting on computers. It's been paid for, and in many cases, annual maintenance is still being paid on this unused software. Before adding any additional technology, it is a good idea to identify and inventory not only what you have but also how the current software is being used. Much like the advanced machining technology that we discovered was not being used on the factory floor, many companies are sitting on a wealth of computer software that may make their work more efficient if they only used it.

DON'T LET THE NAYSAYERS HOLD YOU BACK

I touched on this point earlier and it bears repeating: it is sometimes difficult to persuade people to use technology, particularly advanced technology, that fundamentally changes how they do their work. There is always a fear that their skill set will be eliminated by technology. But you cannot let this resistance deter you from moving into the future.

In the last few years, the global economy has changed dramatically, particularly in the United States. Previously it was relatively easy to find good employees. Now the tables have turned, and it's getting harder and harder to find employees with the skills that companies need. These needs are frequently based on traditional jobs and have not been reinvented using technology. New employees are expecting at least the same level of technology that they have at home. These expectations are not unreasonable, and unless they are met, companies will find it more and more challenging to attract and keep new employees.

Even if there is a reluctance among current employees to embrace technology, this needs to be overcome to prepare the ground for a new wave of employees that have grown up with technology. Applying the same methodology used in the previous steps, simplification, observation, and change will produce a dramatic change in direction and start to create a vision of the future. The introduction of any major piece of technology needs to be shared with all employees along with the rationale for making that investment. New technology sends a vivid message that the company is looking to the future, has a future, and is no longer living in the past.

One of the most dramatic examples of this experience was in the Belgian company mentioned earlier. No new investments in equipment had been made on the shop floor since the company launched nine years earlier. Even worse, they had started off with used surplus equipment from their parent company, Fabrique Nationale. The equipment was poorly maintained, totally out of date, and certainly gave the impression that this division was Fabrique Nationale's poor cousin. I was determined to change this direction and met with the local bank, Bank Brussels Lambert.

As an aside, this was one of the most interesting bank meetings I've ever attended. The meeting started upstairs from the main banking lobby in a boardroom that had a luxurious adjacent dining room. The boardroom had a very comfortable seating area where everybody met prior to lunch. I was advised by my bank contact not to discuss business until after lunch. The purpose of the meeting was for them to get to know me. This is a very different process than currently used by banks in the US and the UK. After a long discussion about my hopes and vision for the company, and my vision for the Walloon area of Belgium, we finished a very elaborate lunch accompanied by some very fine wines. We adjourned to the comfortable sitting area and began to discuss the need for funding new technology on the shop floor. It came as a big surprise when I was informed by the director of the bank that the loan for our equipment upgrade had already been approved. He told me the bank had been observing the turnaround and wanted to be able to contribute to our success. One of the junior bank officers would be visiting me the following day to sign the formal papers. This was without doubt the most enjoyable bank meeting I've ever had.

The purpose of this story is to provide the backdrop for what happened next. For the first time in the history of the company, new state-of-the-art machine tools were being ordered. There was about a four-month lead time before they arrived, and rather than just install them when they were delivered, I decided this was a pivotal moment in the company that should be shared by everybody. An elaborate ceremony was planned that included an invitation to the minister of finance in the Belgian government. To my surprise, he accepted, and asked if a number of other Belgian politicians could also be invited. We, of course, extended invitations to them as well as to all employees and their families. We included all our customers and all our suppliers and even our industrial next-door neighbors. Over two hundred people came to the ceremony, and for the first time there was genuine excitement about the company's future.

We all took great pleasure in getting rid of the old equipment. This was our way of burning the ships like Cortés did when he arrived in Mexico from Spain. There was no way back; we were now enthusiastically committed and moving towards the future. With new technology properly implemented, the company marched quickly towards profitability and enjoyment.

STEP 9

INVENTORY AND EQUIPMENT VALUATION AND ASSESSMENT

"Oh, what a tangled web we weave / When first we practice to deceive," Sir Walter Scott's famous line from his 1808 poem *Marmion: A Tale of Flodden Field* sums up exactly what happens with inventory. At first glance there should be nothing simpler than inventory, but as I outline in the appendix, what starts out as very simple soon becomes a maze of complexity that few people in an organization even understand. In fact, most companies have to retain an accounting firm to help them with valuations of inventory to meet GAAP. The valuation is like a piece of soap in the shower: every time you think you have hold of it, it slips out of your grip. Two people can come up with widely different inventory valuations depending on the method used. This has a direct impact on not only profits but also bank covenants and borrowing certificates. Not having a firm grasp of inventory value can produce disastrous results. In a company that is in financial trouble, this is normally where the bodies are buried. Most items on the balance sheet are reasonably easy to verify. Inventory value is more opaque. A further wrinkle with inventory is that it's frequently used as collateral for bank borrowing. Banks normally limit the borrowing to at most 50% of the value. This should give you a good idea of what they think the value is likely to be in a liquidation scenario.

The starting point in Step 9 is to locate where the inventory is physically stored. This would seem a straightforward task—but again: there are wrinkles. For example: goods in transit. Are they or are they not part of the inventory? Have these items been paid for? If so, is the cost already on the books even if they are not physically in the warehouse? Normally these items do not represent a big percentage of the total company inventory. But if they do, further detective work is required to explain why there is so much value that can't be physically verified. I had a company many years ago that manipulated their profits and bank borrowing by artificially increasing goods in transit, which could not be quickly verified. The mystical value was used when additional collateral value was needed or profits needed to be increased.

In the turnaround of a company that has inventory, it is pivotal to nail down the value of the inventory. It impacts every aspect of the company and can significantly disguise the company's true operating condition. Once inventory is located, it is time for a visit. Inventory counts are normally done over a weekend when there is no movement of inventory in or out. It's always advisable to have with you the employee with granular knowledge of the inventory. Frequently it's an employee who has been with the company a long time and knows where the bodies are buried. If they have worked in the warehouse for much of that time, they are intimately familiar with the inventory. They know which items move and which items have had no movement and therefore represent very little value.

GET TO THE TRUTH ABOUT YOUR INVENTORY

There are three types of inventory you need to be aware of: raw materials, work in progress (WIP), and finished goods. Raw materials are fairly self-explanatory and, as discussed in the appendix, easy to count and easy to value because you know what you paid for them plus any freight costs to bring them into your company. WIP is work you have started but not yet completed, which is valued by the percentage completion. Finished goods are goods that are completed and ready to ship; their value is all the costs that have accumulated during the manufacturing cycle.

A simple multiplication of the quantity times the value gives you a good indication of your inventory's total value. This is very straightforward if the company is a distributor or a retail outlet. If they are a manufacturer, it is a little more complicated.

Calculating inventory value within a manufacturing company is challenging but not impossible. To start, as part of

Step 2, ask the CFO when they did their last inventory count. This can be very revealing because frequently it is an annual event and many months could have gone by since a physical inventory was last done. It is also a good idea to ask the CFO or controller what the variance was between the actual count and what was showing on the books. Almost invariably, this requires a write-down. Applying the percentage write-down to the current inventory value gives you a sense of the current value. It is also important to look at which of the three inventory areas the write-down came from. In most cases, it is WIP because the percentage completion is very difficult to calculate. If the write-down is in finished goods, the problem is more serious, and you need to question why the product was manufactured in the first place if it is currently being written down.

Massive losses can be hidden during the year by overvaluing inventory. The true picture is revealed only after the year-end physical inventory count is completed, valuation is done, and profit, or loss, determined. A company could have been losing money for a year before they find out.

Many companies are extremely reluctant to keep accurate numbers because it is easier to be in a state of denial aided and abetted by inaccurate inventory valuation. Such valuation is based on multiplying the cost times the quantity. LIFO (last in, first out) and FIFO (first in, first out) adjustments are additional accounting methods that try to obtain an accurate valuation by looking at how long items have been in inventory. Each accountant will give you a different way of calculating the inventory valuation. My favorite is FISH—first in, still here—to describe slow-moving inventory (this is not a term used in accounting). The glossary on page 221 lists accounting terms, with more detailed descriptions.

After all this hard work, you have a new number but no one quite knows where it came from. It may be temporarily comforting to the C-suite to see profits, but this is like the man who jumps from a fifty-storey building and as he passes the twentieth floor, says, "I'm doing alright so far." The financial illness is deeply imbedded and completely hidden. It highlights all the normal symptoms of worsening cash flow, only temporarily mitigated by bank borrowing. This is why it is vital for the turnaround person to get the most accurate numbers possible as quickly as possible, especially regarding inventory.

Because inventory count and valuation are so important, it is probably a good time to not only do your own cycle count but also make this a monthly process going forward. Cycle counts are a way of quickly verifying that what is physically in inventory matches what is on the books. The best approach is to start with the 80/20 rule. Start with the inventory items that have the most value. In many cases, 80% of the value is tied up in 20% of the items in each of the three categories—raw materials, WIP, and finished goods—so count those first. Get your guidance from the employee who has granular knowledge of the inventory. They will be eager to point out items that they have been concerned about for years.

I have had many situations where inventory observations indicated really deep-seated problems that had to be addressed immediately. One company had very straightforward inventory as a distributor of high-valued products. A quick count multiplied by the laid-in cost gave me a number after a few hours. When I completed this, I asked the warehouse manager if I could visit their other warehouse since the value I had was half the value on their books. The only possible explanation was that there were two warehouses. I was shocked when he told me this was their only warehouse. I knew instantly I had a problem that dwarfed the operational problems.

My next step was to calmly visit the bookkeeper and hope there was a rational explanation for a $500,000 variance in the inventory value. Equally calmly, she told me that I was completely correct with my valuation and that she had been instructed by the owner to keep two books. To my surprise, she showed me how she took the insurance binder that the bank required to confirm that the inventory was insured and increased this amount to match the books. With a straight face, she also told me that the owner of the company had told her there was no point in paying for insurance on inventory that was not there. This seemed perfectly logical to her. Her method was simple, she took the amount typed on the insurance binder, whited it out (that ages me a bit), typed in the fictitious amount and sent it to the bank to meet their collateral borrowing requirements. Cool, calm fraud. No wonder the owner was nervous about me doing an inventory check.

When confronted with this, the owner immediately blamed his outside accounting firm and denied any knowledge of what was going on. The outside accounting firm that had provided audited statements to the bank decided the best form of defense was to go on the offense. The senior partner in the accounting firm demanded to know my qualifications to do accounting work and whether I had a CPA designation. I told him I did not have the traditional background and qualifications but had learned all the skills required for addition and multiplication in elementary school. The following day, the CPA firm sent in a team that completely verified my numbers. It also transpired that they had found the inventory discrepancy in previous years and were trying to eliminate the variance by reducing the profit each year. The problem was, however, that the company was not making a profit so there was no financial reservoir to draw from.

In a future book, I will describe how the situation was eventually resolved, but it required the dexterity and touch of solving a Rubik's Cube blindfolded. As it turned out, all stakeholders came out whole and no one went to jail. This was a wild adventure but a great teaching moment.

Another company I worked with that had an inventory quandary was a manufacturer in the electronics business. Their inventory of components had high value but only if used in their products. When I isolated where the bulk of the inventory value was stored, I visited the warehouse and asked to see these items. The inventory manager quickly ran his finger over the top of the boxes to show me the amount of dust on them. It was obvious from his expression that he felt they were worthless and immediately explained their origin. These items had been bought for a large contract that was terminated earlier than expected. The large amount of inventory had been purchased to secure a significant quantity discount, which made all the items they had sold more profitable. Unfortunately, when they had to write off the left-over inventory, the profits were replaced with massive losses. Again, inventory value had given temporary comfort to the owners and hidden the fact that the company was losing a lot of money on a monthly basis. The inventory value had been used as collateral to enable increased borrowing from the bank to cover their losses.

After further examination of the inventory value, it became obvious that its value had been further exaggerated intentionally to cover losses. The bank had gone along with the increased borrowing because the company was growing. Now we had to fall on our sword, meet with the bank, and hope they didn't come after the owners for fraud. Luckily, I had established a good reputation with their bank, which was willing to let me work with the company on a turnaround and eventually sell it to a competitor. By the skin of their teeth, the bank, creditors, and owners came out whole.

Hopefully these illustrations highlight the importance of inventory calculation and the enormous impact it has on a business. When infamous bank robber Willie Sutton was asked why he robbed banks, his answer was simple: "Because that's where the money is." The same principle applies to inventory. Not only is that where the money is but it is also the perfect graveyard for the bodies you don't want found.

EQUIPMENT ASSESSMENT AND REPLACEMENT

Equipment assessment, especially in a manufacturing company, helps highlight the vision of the company's future. Your first step is to go through all the equipment on the assets list. That list can be found in the balance sheet as fixed assets. These always come with a deduction for deprecation so the value is net of the depreciation. The challenge here is that the value of the assets can be higher or lower than the amount on the balance sheet because the value on the balance sheet reflects its accounting value not its market value. It is worth paying for an outside appraisal if there is a lot of equipment involved. This will quickly give you not only its market value but also an appraisal of the equipment's condition.

As you get into equipment assessments, I want to call out depreciation and the perils of earnings before interest, tax, and depreciation (EBITDA). I mention this in the appendix as well. The original purpose for depreciation was not to increase current cash flow by reducing taxes. It was designed so a company could sequester money that would be needed to replace worn-out equipment. Instead, depreciation has often been used to artificially increase the value of a company because its valuation was based on a multiple of EBITDA.

This goes a long way to explain why many manufacturing facilities have declined. The main reason was because when they were sold for too much money, there was not enough money left over to replace the equipment. In a turnaround situation, buying new state-of-the-art equipment sends a laser-like signal that the company is worth saving. Once all the new equipment needed has been identified, a plan should be put together to systematically replace all the equipment on a regular basis. Technology is advancing at such a speed that the cost-saving advantages of new equipment totally outweigh the initial costs.

Even if you don't have the funds to buy a lot of new equipment immediately, look at the very generous financing provided by machine tool vendors. Taking advantage of it for a first new machine is at least a start on your replacement program.

Investing in the best equipment sends a wonderful message to all employees that there is a future, and it's bright. The idea that you can muddle along with outdated machines and technology fails in two major areas. Firstly, older equipment uses more manpower to program and run and therefore increases labor costs. Secondly, without new technology you will not find or keep good young employees. They will leave and go to companies that have new technology. This results in high turnover, high retraining costs, and free advertising the company doesn't need (that it's not a good place to work).

The new marketplace—as I've emphasized already but it's worth repeating—is going to be an employees' not an employers' marketplace. Young employees, especially ambitious ones, will only want to work for companies that use advanced technology. They will avoid companies that are still using Windows 3.1 and paper. They will frequently make their employment decisions based on the technology that a company has. A strange transition has occurred that I discuss further in Step 10. The seismic shift that has occurred has created, for the first time in human history, a situation where an individual has more advanced technology in their house than they do at work. The CEO's nine-year-old daughter is more comfortable with her computer and knows more about it than her CEO dad. Companies need the best and most advanced equipment to survive.

I have been through many manufacturing facilities in my life and the average age of equipment is normally fifteen to twenty years. In one recent company I visited, the equipment was more than thirty years old. And guess what? They were finding it impossible to hire people to work on the second and third shifts. Technology has advanced so much in the last fifteen years that companies are light-years behind.

Knowing the average age of major equipment gives you a good indication of what you have to do to make your turnaround lasting and effective. The best examples of this are airlines. The ones with the lowest average age of their fleet always rank near the top in terms of quality of service; those with the highest average age always rank at the bottom. A recent company I have been working with not only had old equipment but also repair work-arounds that put their employees and maintenance people at risk of being killed. Although the company owner was saving money, this could have ended in him going to jail for a long time if one of his employees had been killed (some savings).

This raised a number of red flags, the biggest one being that employees were knowingly put in high-risk situations. The other being shoddy maintenance that indicated how the equipment was treated. In this particular case, the electrical power main switch had been deactivated so that when the power was switched off it continued to run. This lethal and bizarre work-around was done to avoid breaker switches from activating. There is a strange human condition that allows us to think something is safe because there has not been an accident. Texting and driving falls into this category. Sadly, I have seen many examples of this over the years, and it still shocks and sickens me that an owner would be willing to put his employees at risk of being killed or maimed to save a few bucks.

It is important to establish that going forward, the company will not tolerate this sort of behavior. This is a good time to establish a company hotline that can be used anonymously to find out if any of these risks are still out there. Employees are frequently intimidated into covering up for an owner. As the new leader, you must create a safe harbor for them so they will let you know. Caring about their safety and the quality of the equipment sends exactly the message needed to show that there is a new sheriff in town.

A few years ago, when I was doing the final due diligence on acquiring a manufacturing company, I found a very obvious sign that the company needed help and needed it quickly. Right in front of me was a 35-ton press brake. For those not familiar with a press brake, it's a tool that bends metal using the enormous force of a hydraulic fixture coming down on top of the metal. This metal can be up to one-half inch thick. In order to make sure the metal is bent at exactly the right place, there are backstops to limit how deeply you can set the metal into the press. These backstops are moved by the operator with the press brake locked in place. What drew my eye immediately were two wooden chucks at each end of the machine holding the press brake in place. When I asked why they were there, the operator told me that sometimes the platen (weighing 35 tons) comes down without being activated, so his safety measure was to put in the wooden blocks so he wouldn't lose his hands. When I asked how long it had been like that, he told me years. I asked him why it had not been repaired, and he told me it was because the company had no money. The owner was willing to put his employees at risk to save money. This was the message being sent. After I bought the company, my first action was to ceremoniously remove the equipment and replace it with a brand-new press brake. No more wooden chucks.

To understand the quality of the equipment, a quick visit to the maintenance engineer's office will tell you everything. If it is messy and disorganized, with poor tools, that will be reflected in the condition of the equipment. There should be a maintenance schedule for every piece of equipment. There should also be a detailed record of all prior repairs and maintenance, with the root cause of each repair identified. This can be a big reveal. When looking at an analysis of repairs, I found that those for one machine comprised 50% of our repairs each month. Money was lost not only with downtime and loss of production but also with the accumulated costs of the repairs. A brand-new machine could have been bought years ago, eliminating both issues.

Financing the Changes Needed

What if you need to buy equipment but you do not have the money? One positive factor with machine tools is that they have a remarkable record of retaining their value. The better the equipment, the longer the time between purchase and delivery. This sets up an interesting dynamic that provides perfect security for financing even 100% of the equipment cost. In many cases, good equipment retains its purchase price for a couple of years. If you did have to sell a relatively new machine in the first two years, you can frequently get more than you paid for it, in part because you can offer immediate delivery rather than the purchaser having to wait up to nine months if buying directly from the manufacturer. Equipment vendors offer up to 100% financing if asked, together with low interest rates and deferred payments that do not start until the equipment is fully operational and earning money. This provides great incentive and minimal risk to replace virtually everything in the factory that is older than a few years. As part of your turnaround, new equipment shows everyone what the future is going to look like. In one company, I had a new piece of equipment come in every month for the first year. When the delivery dates were confirmed, we stopped production and shared with all the employees what the new machine was going to do, how much better it was than what it replaced, and how it was going to make the company more competitive. This process created positive anticipation for the monthly arrivals and great momentum during the first year of the turnaround. The main message was that our employees deserved the best equipment and we were going to provide them with it. The simple act of getting everyone together for arrival of the equipment reinforced that message.

SMALL GESTURES MEAN A LOT

Small gestures frequently have a disproportionate impact, both positive and negative. On the positive side, smiling and saying thank you come to mind. It is up to the company leadership to constantly reinforce the message of employee respect. This is not to be confused with creating an environment of low expectations. It's exactly the opposite. You set high expectations, but you also provide the tools to make meeting, even exceeding, those expectations feasible. Very small gestures can tell you a lot about a company. I recently visited a company called Renishaw in rural Gloucester, UK. This was their global headquarters and about a three-hour drive from London. Given the narrow lanes and the need to drive on the right-hand side of the road, I decided to have a driver take me. Upon arrival, I checked in with reception; they knew who I was, and I was warmly greeted. The receptionist asked if I had had a driver bring me down from London, and I told her I had. She then asked if I could bring him to the reception area. When I brought him in, she let him know that there was a more comfortable area for him to wait in the building. Knowing that I was going to be there all day, she also gave him vouchers for lunch. This small gesture told me everything I needed to know about the company and its wonderful founder, Sir David McMurtry. Here is a company doing close to a billion dollars in sales, with an owner who is a billionaire in his own right, still concerned that drivers are comfortable when they visit their headquarters.

AS YOU TACKLE Step 9, here is a recap of the essential steps you'll take:

- Inventory and inspect all the equipment the company currently owns.

- Identify which equipment, if replaced, will have the biggest impact.

- Get recommendations from the people actually running the machines.

- Plan and show everyone the replacement schedule and let them get excited about the future.

STEP 10

COMPANY PRESENTATION OF THE GO-FORWARD PLAN

This is it! Step 10 is where you reveal your vision for the company's future to the entire team. This vision incorporates all the input gained from the company meetings collated into one powerful presentation document. For example, the plan for new equipment is outlined and respective brochures are included; detailed architectural plans are drawn up to show everyone what the company will look like in a few years.

Dates and accountability are a critical part of this presentation. You only earn credibility by doing what you say you will do, when you said you would do it. If for some reason part of the plan changes or dates are not going to be met, everyone needs to be informed at the earliest opportunity. Even with careful selection of employees, there will always be some doubting Thomases, and it is important not to give them any ammunition. If planned items happen sooner than expected, this also has to be communicated. Keeping everybody informed creates the momentum you need. A company in trouble develops a malaise. This can only be eliminated by an exciting vision of the future materializing and everybody recognizing their part in making it happen.

As we've covered, anything that resembles the old way has to be removed or changed. This can be very difficult. Sometimes something radical has to be implemented. It needs to be a dramatic demonstration that significant changes have been made and there will be no going back to the way it was before.

If part of the plan includes a move to a new facility, it is worthwhile to invest in a high-quality visual presentation of what the new facility is going to look like. Thirty years ago, when I was doing an early turnaround, I engaged a firm of architects to put together a visualization of what the new company would look like. With the technology available today, it's possible to build a fully animated virtual facility that employees can walk through so they can appreciate and anticipate exactly what their future is going to be.

By this step in the company transition, all employee reductions have been made and you are speaking to those who are on the turnaround team. As emphasized earlier, it's very important that major employee reductions be done once, and only once, and that the remaining team members are notified that this is the last major employee reduction that will take place. The employees should be told that their former colleagues were good employees; unfortunately, like a football team, a company is limited to a specific number of people who can play on the team. It is important to convince employees that they do not have to look over their shoulder and wonder when the next shoe is going to drop. If this is not done, it is impossible to get the level of productivity needed: there will be a temptation for employees to organize work in a way that will make them indispensable. As part of your presentation, identify and thank individuals who have made valuable recommendations. It needs to be emphasized that the plan was a team effort and success will come because of that. This is also a good time to open up for questions to address any lingering concerns.

Moving forward, communications need to be on an individual basis or in small groups. In addition to your presentation, setting up this new normal is a big focus of Step 10.

COMMUNICATE AND MAKE ALL CHANGES VISIBLE

A critical part of Step 10 is implementing a process of regular communication with all employees. Management by walking around (more on this below) can demonstrate that you care about the outcome of every employee. Employees who work on different shifts or in areas that management never visits welcome an impromptu visit. One time I turned up at three in the morning to meet those working the graveyard shift. The impact was profound. They had never seen anyone from management before, and many had worked for the company for years.

There is always a great temptation for companies to have endless meetings, but meetings can be the biggest theft of company time. The best are stand-ups: short, focused meetings. Begin each by identifying the reason for the meeting and what you feel will be gained by having it.

Prior to my arrival in one turnaround, the company had hired a consultant to help them get back on track. One of their problems was meetings. There were so many meetings that people were scheduling multiple meetings at the same time. The consultant felt this needed to be better organized, so he bought software to manage everyone's schedule of meetings. He also felt that the meetings would be more effective if they had a pre-meeting to discuss what was going to be discussed in the actual meeting. To add to the overload of meetings, he also suggested that people have a post-meeting to reaffirm what they had learned in the meeting. Needless to say, when I started with the company his consulting assignment came to an abrupt halt.

Meetings in general need to be short and have a purpose. Better communication can be done on a one-on-one basis or in small groups. When organizing a meeting, make sure only those people who are going to benefit from the meeting attend.

Communications is an ongoing process. The phrase "management by walking around" is very applicable. It is very reassuring for employees to have a constant reminder that the ship has a captain and that person enjoys steering the ship. As the leader, you are watched and scrutinized all the time. What you may think is unimportant can be misread by an employee and misinterpreted. The power of constant communication and constant reassurance is by far the best way to keep the turnaround momentum going.

Successful changes need to be highlighted and their benefits constantly reinforced. There needs to be early intervention on any backsliding or retreating back to the old ways. It takes a while for the momentum that you have created to be self-sustaining, so during the transition you need to be the constant cheerleader. It means not ignoring, avoiding, or hiding problems like the previous administration. It means acknowledging, confronting, and intervening to eliminate issues promptly. Very few problems get better on their own, and it is far easier to resolve a nascent problem than one that has metastasized.

Companies are a delicate organism and need to be constantly nurtured and reinvigorated. They do not run on autopilot and require a significant amount of energy and direction to continually advance. Companies that have had financial problems have scar tissue. It is important, through communications, to make sure that past treatment of employees is permanently consigned to the history book.

CONCLUSION

BURN THE SHIPS
À LA CORTÉS

Hernán Cortés was a Spanish conquistador who led an expedition to Mexico in 1519. Upon arrival, he faced opposition from the Indigenous Peoples. With some members of his own expedition reluctant to continue, Cortés famously ordered the burning of his ships. According to some accounts, the decision came after a group of soldiers attempted to mutiny and return to Cuba. He is said to have watched the sinking vessels while telling his troops, "We now have no choice but to succeed."

The decision to burn the ships was a bold one: his troops had no way to retreat or return to Spain. Cortés was effectively committing himself and his men to the conquest of Mexico, making it clear that there was no turning back.

While Cortés's decision was a risky one, it ultimately proved successful. By eliminating the possibility of retreat, he forced his troops to focus all their efforts on achieving their goal of conquering Mexico. Despite facing overwhelming odds, Cortés and his army ultimately defeated the Aztec Empire and established Spanish control over the region. I have always used the story of Cortés and the burning of his ships as a metaphor for commitment.

Significant change is frequently elastic. In other words, the bigger or more dramatic the change, the greater the tendency to revert to the previous state. All the outstanding things that you accomplished in the 10 Steps can easily go back to the way they were. The trick is to burn the ships like Cortés. You need to make sure that the routes back to the previous state are eliminated. This means that overall company improvement must continue, and on a regular basis.

Companies need to continuously self-examine themselves in relation to their competitors, their suppliers, and their employees. This is not one and done, but an ongoing process that needs to be embedded in the company culture. The phrase "things only get easier when you're going downhill" is very true. Being in business is tough. Business is one of the last areas of survival of the fittest. Even companies that survive a near-death experience are always vulnerable if they take their eye off the ball. Luckily the ball is very easy to watch. The ball is the financial condition and must be watched like a hawk. Financial statements need to be honest and reflect what is happening not what you might like to have happen. Financial deception occurs very frequently in start-ups. To convince a budding entrepreneur to continue, or even to start, there is often a need to create over-ambitious numbers. In addition, there is a need to convince benefactors (venture capitalists) to continue pouring money into the ill-fated ventures. Recent upheavals in Silicon Valley have highlighted this, and unlike in previous periods, like the dot-com boom, principals in these companies are being held legally responsible for what is outright fraud. One of the most recent glaring examples of this was Elizabeth Holmes and her company Theranos Inc. Particularly stunning was how long it took for anybody to question what the courts decided was complete fraud. This wasn't a case of a valiant entrepreneur trying to find a solution, but more outright deception.

It takes courage to perform a detailed operational and financial audit on your company, but if you do it on a frequent basis you will avoid being a casualty in a world that has many business casualties. Long-term survivors are few. Bright candles burn out quickly. Sales growth is a great seducer, especially in the early years of a company. But unless the sales growth is accompanied by growth in profits, you will have no seed corn to plant for the next harvest. Bootstrapping a company (i.e., providing your own funding) is considered old fashioned and has been replaced by the turbocharging impact of venture capital and private equity. Unfortunately, this can postpone the day of reckoning or the ability to determine whether a company has any long-term viability at all. The days of get-rich-quick schemes and desperate searches for unicorns are hopefully coming to an end. The unearned funding power of a company—otherwise known as other people's money—distorts a company's viability and creates legions of zombie companies.

A remarkable coincidence is that virtually all companies run out of money after their first six months. If a company starts with $10 million, they have nice offices, lots of people, a refrigerator filled with food for all their employees, and six months later, they've spent their money. If they start with $1 million, they have smaller offices, fewer employees, a mini fridge, and they run out of money after six months. Surviving those early years is an excellent litmus test and a good forecaster for long-term survival.

STEWARDSHIP AND SUSTAINABILITY

I've left the importance of stewardship until this last chapter. No one owns a business: you are a steward of that business for a limited time. Stewardship involves care and consideration for the future. Like a farmer, you need to take care of the soil. If you overuse or abuse it, you will deplete its value and limit its future productivity. The ethics that you cultivate in a business are part of being a steward. Making sure that your successors share similar values is a vital part of your succession.

If stewardship is handled well, the longevity of the company and your mentorship will be your legacy. If not, everyone's work and effort will be consigned to the garbage can of history. When you look at the extraordinary amount of life energy—and the very high percentage of waking hours—that people put into the creation and maintenance of a company, it is tragic to see its disappearance through greed, incompetence, and dishonesty. As the steward you can have an enormous impact on employees' happiness and well-being. In many cases, depression and anxiety have their roots in miserable and unfulfilling jobs. This is often accompanied by unnecessary stress inflicted by supervisors and company owners. Treat everyone the way you wish to be treated and you will make a major contribution to everyone's mental health.

One of the current buzzwords is sustainability. A company's sustainability provides many people with the ability to take care of their families. This responsibility should not be taken lightly. This does not mean that you take no risks. Business in itself is risky. The trick is to avoid making it even riskier by unnecessarily gambling with a company's future.

When it comes to business longevity and how a business can survive for centuries, there is no better example than Nishiyama Hot Spring, Keiunkan, an inn located in Yamanashi Prefecture in Japan. It is the oldest continuously traded family company that is still in business and was founded in 705 AD. It has been run by the same family for over 1,300 years, making it the oldest family business in the world.

Nishiyama Hot Spring, Keiunkan has survived wars, natural disasters, and social upheavals. The hot springs are said to have healing properties, and the inn has welcomed many famous guests over the centuries, including samurai war-riors, shoguns, and even the Japanese imperial family. The hot spring inn has thirty-seven rooms and offers traditional Japanese hospitality, including kaiseki cuisine, which is a multi-course meal featuring local ingredients.

This is a wonderful example of sustainability and high-lights the care and stewardship that must have been necessary for a company to last over a thousand years.

Business is a fascinating journey that incorporates all aspects of human nature. Like everything in life, there is an element of luck but there are also many ways to reduce risks. Honest assessment is the key to not only long-term survival but also a level of enjoyment that comes from operating a business well. Constantly worrying and wondering when the next blow will land is not an enjoyable experience. Be honest with yourself, be honest with your employees, be honest with your bank and your investors, be honest with your suppliers, be honest with your customers, be honest with friends and family. Deceiving yourself and everyone around you achieves nothing except the buying of time. You don't have a lot of time in life, and pretending to be something you are not is the ultimate waste of time.

If you abide by this and have some luck, you will create an incredibly enjoyable journey for yourself and your fellow trav-elers. And you will understand the true romance of commerce.

APPENDIX

FINANCIAL PRIMER

PUTTING TOGETHER A FINANCIAL STATEMENT

Accounting elements are very straightforward and apply to any company, whether a small retail shop or a complex manufacturing operation. Here are the basic elements you need to understand when looking at a financial statement related to a turnaround:

A = Sales

B = Cost of sales

C = Direct labor

D = Direct materials

E = Outshop processes (adding surface finishes to metal anodize, paint, etc.)

F = Gross margin

G = Manufacturing overhead

H = Administrative costs

I = Net profit before taxes

Using these elements, specific equations produce the financial information you need about your company. At this point, it is all addition and subtraction, skills you mastered in elementary school. Don't be fooled into thinking that business financials are anything more than basic arithmetic.

(C + D + E) – (G + H) = I (net profit before taxes)

C + D + E = B (cost of sales)

A – B = F (gross margin)

A – B – G – H = I (net profits before taxes)

The above calculations result in categories, or type of account, with subcategories, which, when listed together, are called the chart of accounts. The chart of accounts is a description of these subcategories (see sample on page 217).

When an expense is entered into the books, it is put in a specific category and subcategory. Most accounting systems do this automatically since a particular expense is almost always put in the same account; e.g., rent will always go in the rent account in the chart of accounts.

Putting together a good chart of accounts is more art than science. You need to have enough detail to be able to do a competent analysis but not so many accounts that the overall picture gets lost in the detail. Also, if a chart of accounts is too detailed, there is a greater chance that an amount may be put into the wrong account.

When I started doing turnarounds almost fifty years ago, I had three items I always used to focus on, all of which I think are still relevant today.

1. **Open all the mail.** Today you need to add gaining access to all the CFO's and a previous CEO's email.

2. **Sign and approve all checks and payments to get a hold of where the money is going out of the company**. Look at the section on source and application of funds. This report will give you a complete analysis of where the money's coming from and where it's going and can predict significant cash shortages that may be awaiting the company.

3. **Ask to see all expenses related to professional services**. This is where any issues of litigation, tax, HR issues and disputes will be found. In one company I found details of an ongoing issue with the Environmental Protection Agency (EPA), where the legal costs had been fully covered by insurance. This coverage was about to be exhausted as we had reached the limits of the coverage and needed to settle the claim or be stuck with untenable additional legal costs.

These are still very important steps that will allow you to make significant progress on Day 1.

PAYING ATTENTION TO TWO KEY TERMS

As part of your overall accounting education, it is important to learn two other terms frequently used in the accounting world: **EBIDTA** and **source and application of funds.**

EBITDA stands for earnings before interest, taxes, depreciation, and amortization. It first apperaed in the 1970s when investor John Malone was growing his cable and media giant Tele-Communications, Inc. He felt that EBITDA represented a better way to value a company than the traditional earnings after taxes method. Unfortunately, his methodology crept into the accounting lexicon and has resulted in grossly overvaluing companies and disguising their true performance. One group that adopted EBITDA very rapidly was merger and acquisition companies. EBITDA allowed them to overvalue companies they were selling by creating a valuation based on a multiple of EBITDA (5 × EBITDA). Guess who benefited most from this? Certainly not the buyer of company. Famed investor Warren Buffett has always been adamantly against using EBITDA. If your company uses it as a metric, you need to get rid of it as soon as possible. It dangerously distorts the financial picture.

Remarkably for an accounting term, **source and application of funds** is exactly what it says it is. The source: where the funds come from. The application: where the funds go. There are some accounting nuances (surprise, surprise) that can make it more complicated, but it is a very valuable report to see how healthy the company is from a cash standpoint.

Sometimes cash just seems to disappear: an example of this is when customers slow down on paying their bills; an increase in what you are owed does not impact your profitability but . can eliminate your cash. On the other hand, occasionally cash just appears: for example, when you don't pay your bills, you will have a temporary increase in cash. Some big companies use this to increase their liquidity by paying suppliers in 90 days rather than 30 days. Increasing the amount of inventory in the company can frequently cause liquidity problems. All these things can happen at once, so it is very important to look at net changes to determine what is increasing and what is decreasing. Look at it as taking the company's temperature to ensure everything is in check: this report can identify if a fever is raging or abating. It can also confirm whether your turnaround changes are producing the desired results. Cash is your lifeblood. so focusing on your bank balance is always a good idea. Generating and preserving cash are the primary goals of a turnaround.

BALANCE SHEET

The balance sheet is the easiest part of your financial sleuthing and is a treasure trove of information. Your balance sheet is essentially an overview of the company's assets and liabilities (see glossary for definitions on page 221). The formula is very simple and again applies to small and very large companies. Both the assets and liabilities are separated into short-term and long-term categories: the former materializing in 12 months; the latter beyond 12 months. An example of this categorization is a five-year loan to the bank for $1,000,000: $200,000 is considered a current liability with the balance of $800,000 being a long-term liability. Putting together the balance sheet this way gives you an idea of whether you have the resources in the next year to cover your liabilities. The technical term for this is **current ratio**. A good current ratio is 3:1, which means your assets are 3 times your liabilities. A company that has a ratio of less than 1:1 is technically insolvent. This means that they do not have the funds to meet their obligations for the following 12 months. Banks almost always incorporate a current ratio requirement into their borrowing covenants. A caveat here is that not all current assets are easy to liquidate. You may not be able to collect all the money that is owed you. If you have any doubts, the accounts receivable need to be reduced by the amount you do not expect to get paid. This is put in a category of doubtful accounts and this amount needs to be subtracted from the accounts receivable total. Inventory is treated as a current asset, but if it is not salable within 12 months then this needs to also be reflected with a reduced inventory valuation (see page 175 for more about inventory valuation).

When you add up everything you own and subtract everything you owe, hopefully you have a positive number representing your net worth. Again. Elementary math. Here is that basic and important equation:

A = Assets

B = Liabilities

C = Net worth

$A - B = C$

But the devil is in the details, meaning a close look at three categories of assets and how are they valued. The value of the first category, **cash**, is self-explanatory: it is the amount of money you have in the bank. Valuation of the other two—accounts receivable and inventory—can be more complex.

Accounts Receivable

This is money you are owed by your customers. The gray area in determining the accurate value of your accounts receivable is in whether you get paid what you are currently owed. If you feel there is any doubt that you are going to be paid by any customer, it is essential that you discount the value of the accounts receivable. This is reflected on a balance sheet as accounts receivables minus doubtful accounts.

Customers that are not paying provide you with an excellent source of information about the company you are trying to turn around. By finding out why they are not paying, you are able to quickly assess where there are significant problems affecting your company. Are your products defective? Why are the customers not paying? This intelligence is very valuable when making operational improvements. On the other side of this transaction, one of the most frequent reasons for not paying is that the customer does not have the money. The financial strength of your customers is vital in determining whether you are going to get paid. Did they buy product from your company because their existing suppliers stopped shipping due to nonpayment? Taking on your competitors' poor-paying customers does both of them a great favor, but in the process damages your company.

Do you have current financial statements on your customers? Have you done a recent credit check? I emphasize recent because many companies do an initial credit check but do not update on a regular basis. It is essential when assessing the true value of accounts receivable that you look at the aging. This is normally reported as currently owed within the payment terms, 30 days past the terms, 60 days past the terms, 90 days past the terms, and over 90 days. The terms of payment may vary between customers so this report can understate the problem, especially if overly generous terms are given. For instance, if 90-day terms are offered and a customer is showing 90 days past due, you have extended them credit for 6 months. A lot can go wrong in your customer's business in 6 months. In the meantime, you are financing this lack of cash flow. Offering an early-payment discount is a very valuable way of speeding up your cash flow.

The value of your accounts receivable is only as good as the customers' ability to pay. Nonpayment can have a very negative impact on your business. You already have all the cost in making or buying the product and now you end up getting nothing for it. It obviously would have been better not to have had the customer at all. This truth always reminds me of the famous line in Ernest Hemingway's book *The Sun Also Rises.* When the owner of a business is asked how he went bankrupt, he replies, "Two ways. Gradually and then suddenly." When your customers go bankrupt, it is all of a sudden. It is best to take this into consideration and have a very aggressive initial write-down of accounts receivable until you are absolutely certain you are going to get paid the amount recorded. If not done, you are basing your company's future on hope, which is not a good business strategy.

In the same category as accounts receivable are notes receivable. This is also money you are owed. A note receivable is paid over time and has interest accrued. The same principles apply to these notes. Is the noteholder financially viable? Are they paying as per the agreed-upon terms? If the answers are "yes" and "yes," then you can leave them on the balance sheet; if not, they need to be removed.

KEEPING ITEMS ON the balance sheet, particularly assets that you know are not going to materialize, is the ultimate form of financial deception and only kicks the day of reckoning down the road. Eventually it has to be addressed so there is no time like the present, particularly in a turnaround scenario.

Another nebulous item on the balance sheet that needs to be removed immediately because it has no bearing on the true valuation of the company is the item called goodwill. Frequently, when a company purchases a new company the purchase price exceeds the net book value of the purchased company. In order to balance the balance sheet, the difference is called goodwill.

Inventory

The value of inventory is the murkiest value of all. It is very difficult to accurately calculate not only because of the many moving parts but also because of the valuation method created by accounting and tax considerations. In its simplest terms—if you are, for instance, in retail or distribution—what you paid for an item including shipping is called your landed cost. Multiply that figure by the number of items purchased and you have the value. If the price you paid has increased due to inflationary pressures on that group of items, make sure to reflect what you actually paid. Your margin is created by the difference between what you paid for item and what you eventually sell it for.

The real complexity comes when trying to value the inventory in a manufacturing business. Different types of inventories and valuations that can fluctuate make finding the real value a challenge.

The following walks you through those unique considerations to get the most accurate assessment of where the company is financially before you create a recovery strategy. You do not want to implement a plan and find out later that assets, in particular inventory, were overstated and liabilities were understated. For the record, in fifty years of doing company turnarounds, I only found one example of understated assets or overstated liabilities. This was a steel distributor who aggressively wrote down his inventory value to reduce his taxes. Unfortunately, he died suddenly, and his wife put the company up for sale—for its book value, which was a fraction of its real worth. Luckily, the buyer had integrity and made sure the wife received the real worth of the company. Food for thought.

Inventory in a manufacturing company is broken up into three categories:

1. Raw materials
2. Work in progress
3. Finished goods

Value of **raw materials** is straightforward: it is the landed cost, as described above, multiplied by the quantity of material. Where the valuation gets a bit more complicated is determining whether you have any outstanding orders for this material. The material itself has the value based on what you paid for it; however, if you have no need for it and it cannot be returned, its value is only what you can sell it for in the marketplace, which may be lower than its current value in inventory. It also begs the question of why it was purchased in the first place. Finding out why is another piece of valuable information that can be fed into your turnaround plan. Sometimes there are minimum quantity requirements from the vendor in order to get a price break. The price break has no value if you cannot use all the material that was ordered and it has to be scrapped. The original transaction can look profitable, but when you write off unused material, that profit can disappear very rapidly.

Work in progress (WIP) is my favorite inventory category because this is where a lot of bodies are buried. The first thing to recognize is that it's very difficult on a manufacturing floor to calculate the percentage completion of every item you are manufacturing. The best you can do is accurately apply labor costs as they occur. A simple time card system with labor accurately allocated to the cost of the item will give you a reasonable valuation. Unfortunately, this number needs to have manufacturing overhead added to it, which increases its value.

Without getting into the weeds of LIFO (last in, first out) or FIFO (first in, first out) or the ubiquitous FISH (first in, still here; not an accounting term but mine to describe a lot of inventory I have seen over the years), it is always wise to take a very conservative position on the valuation of WIP.

A quick accounting test that will help is determining which is lower: cost or market. Take a few of the most valuable items you are manufacturing, look at the current costs that have been booked against each, determine their percentages of completion, and extrapolate for each what the total cost will be upon completion. Take the current sale price for each item and deduct the respective cost that you have just calculated.

This will give you a value. If the value is negative for any item, i.e., your cost exceeds what you can sell it for, your inventory needs to be reduced in value to reflect this. If the value is positive, this gives you the margin percentage you will eventually get when the product is sold. These steps are fairly time consuming for your first day so it is an excellent task to delegate to the CFO, who in most cases will believe that the true value of the inventory is being established.

Finished goods are exactly what they sound like. The big questions are: Why are there finished goods? Why have they not been shipped to a customer? Another exercise to get you a great indication of the true inventory value is to ask the CFO whether a work order is only started on the shop floor and material ordered when there is a purchase order from the customer. If that is not the case, that means inventory was bought and manufactured on speculation. This can sometimes happen because of economic manufacturing quantities determined by the MRP (material requirements planning) system. The software determines the most economic quantity that needs to be manufactured based on time for setting up the machine and minimum lot charges at an outside processor for surface finish. Unless the company has a long-term agreement (LTA) to support such a commitment, this is a risky strategy and can end up in major inventory write-downs. Even with an LTA, revision levels can change, making the value disappear for parts in inventory.

Example: Chart of Accounts

This chart of accounts includes the different types of accounts needed to calculate a profit and loss statement. The revenue account include sales and service revenue, while the cost of sales account includes cost of goods sold, direct labor costs, and direct materials costs. The gross profit is calculated by subtracting the cost of sales from the revenue.

The operating expenses account includes various expenses such as salaries and wages, rent, utilities, insurance, depreciation and amortization, marketing and advertising, professional fees, office supplies and expenses, travel and entertainment, taxes and licenses, bad debts, and other expenses. The operating profit is calculated by subtracting the total operating expenses from the gross profit.

Other income and expenses such as interest income and expense are also included, and the net profit before and after tax are calculated by subtracting the income tax expense from the operating profit.

Account Type	Account Name
Revenue	Sales
Revenue	Service revenue
Cost of Sales	Cost of goods sold
Cost of Sales	Direct labor costs
Cost of Sales	Direct materials costs
Gross Profit	
Operating Expenses	Salaries and wages
Operating Expenses	Rent
Operating Expenses	Utilities
Operating Expenses	Insurance
Operating Expenses	Depreciation and amortization
Operating Expenses	Marketing and advertising
Operating Expenses	Professional fees
Operating Expenses	Office supplies and expenses
Operating Expenses	Travel and entertainment
Operating Expenses	Taxes and licenses
Operating Expenses	Bad debts
Operating Expenses	Other expenses
Operating Profit	
Other Income	Interest income
Other Expenses	Interest expense
Net Profit Before Taxes	
Income Tax Expense	
Net Profit After Taxes	

Example: Balance Sheet Chart of Accounts

This chart of accounts includes the different types of accounts needed to calculate a balance sheet. The assets section includes accounts for current assets such as cash and cash equivalents, short-term investments, accounts receivable, inventory, pre-paid expenses, and other current assets. Property, plant, and equipment, and intangible assets are also included. The accumulated depreciation account is used to show the cumulative depreciation on property, plant, and equipment. Other assets such as long-term investments and patents are also included.

The liabilities section includes accounts for current liabilities such as accounts payable, accrued expenses, deferred revenue, short-term loans and debt, and other current liabilities. Long-term liabilities such as long-term debt, deferred income taxes, and other long-term liabilities are also included.

The equity section includes accounts for paid-in capital, which shows the amount of capital contributed by shareholders, and retained earnings, which shows the accumulated profits and losses of the company. Treasury stock and accumulated other comprehensive income are also included, as well as other equity accounts.

Account Type	Account Name
Assets	Current Assets
Assets	Cash and Cash Equivalents
Assets	Short-term Investments
Assets	Accounts Receivable
Assets	Inventory
Assets	Prepaid Expenses
Assets	Other Current Assets
Assets	Property, Plant, and Equipment
Assets	Accumulated Depreciation
Assets	Intangible Assets
Assets	Other Assets
Liabilities	Current Liabilities
Liabilities	Accounts Payable
Liabilities	Accrued Expenses
Liabilities	Deferred Revenue
Liabilities	Short-term Loans and Debt
Liabilities	Other Current Liabilities
Liabilities	Long-term Liabilities
Liabilities	Long-term Debt
Liabilities	Deferred Income Taxes
Liabilities	Other Long-term Liabilities
Equity	Paid-in Capital
Equity	Retained Earnings
Equity	Treasury Stock
Equity	Accumulated Other Comprehensive Income
Equity	Other Equity

GLOSSARY

In addition to a definition, some terms include further background information and/or explanations to help you better understand relevance in the context of a turnaround.

Accounts payable Money owed by a business to its suppliers or vendors for goods or services received on credit.

Accounts receivable Money owed to a business by its customers for goods or services sold on credit.

Accruals Revenue or expenses that have been earned or incurred but that have not yet been recorded in the financial statements.

Applications of funds The section of the source and application of funds statement that shows the various uses of cash outflows for the business during the period. It can include:

1. Operating activities, including cash used to pay for the business's day-to-day operations, such as rent, salaries, and other expenses.

2. Investing activities, including cash used to purchase long-term assets, such as property, plant, and equipment, as well as investments in other businesses.

3. Financing activities, including cash used to repay borrowing activities, such as loans and bonds, as well as cash used for equity financing activities, such as stock repurchases or payment of dividends.

The difference between the total sources of funds and the total applications of funds is called the net change in cash. If the net change in cash is positive, it means that the business has generated more cash than it has used during the period. If the net change in cash is negative, it means that the business has used more cash than it has generated during the period.

Assets Resources owned by a business or organization, such as cash, property, or equipment.

Balance sheet A financial statement that shows a business's assets, liabilities, and equity at a specific point in time.

Cash flow statement A financial statement that shows a business's cash inflows and outflows over a period of time.

Chart of accounts A list of all the accounts used by a business or organization to record financial transactions. It provides a standardized way to categorize and organize financial transactions, making it easier to generate financial statements and reports. It typically includes asset accounts, liability accounts, equity accounts, revenue accounts, and expense accounts. Each account is assigned a unique number or code for easy reference, and the accounts are grouped into categories based on their type and function.

Current ratio A financial ratio commonly used to evaluate a company's liquidity, which is the ability of the company to meet its short-term obligations using its current assets.

It is calculated by dividing a company's current assets by its current liabilities. Current assets are those assets that are expected to be converted into cash within one year, such as cash and cash equivalents, marketable securities, accounts receivable, and inventory. Current liabilities are those obligations that are due within one year, such as accounts payable, accrued expenses, and short-term debt.

For example, if a company has current assets of $100,000 and current liabilities of $50,000, the current ratio would be 2:1 ($100,000 / $50,000). This means that the company has twice as many current assets as it has current liabilities, which suggests that it may be able to meet its short-term obligations without difficulty.

The current ratio is important because it provides insight into a company's ability to pay its debts in the short term. Generally, a higher current ratio indicates that a company is in a better position to meet its short-term obligations. However, a very high current ratio may suggest that a company is not efficiently using its current assets or is not investing enough in growth opportunities.

Depreciation The process of allocating the cost of an asset over its useful life.

EBITDA (earnings before interest, taxes, depreciation, and amortization) A financial metric used to evaluate a company's profitability before considering the impact of nonoperating expenses and noncash expenses, such as interest, taxes, depreciation, and amortization.

It is used by investors, analysts, and business owners as a measure of a company's operating performance because it allows them to compare the profitability of companies with different capital structures, tax rates, and accounting methods. It is especially useful for evaluating companies in industries where depreciation and amortization expenses can be significant, such as manufacturing, mining, and telecommunications.

EBITDA is calculated by taking a company's operating income and adding back the depreciation and amortization expenses as well as any nonoperating expenses such as interest and taxes. The formula is: EBITDA = Operating income + Depreciation + Amortization

Some people argue that EBITDA can be misleading because it does not include important expenses like interest, taxes, and capital expenditures. Others believe that it provides a more accurate picture of a company's underlying operating performance than net income or other measures of profitability.

It is important to note that EBITDA should not be used as the only measure of a company's financial performance, as it does not take into account factors such as changes in working capital, debt service requirements, and other nonoperating expenses that can affect a company's overall financial health.

Equity The difference between assets and liabilities, representing the portion of a business that is owned by its shareholders.

Expenses Costs incurred by a business in order to generate revenue, such as rent, salaries, and materials.

FASB (Financial Accounting Standards Board) An independent, private-sector organization based in the United States that establishes and improves financial accounting and reporting standards, known as Generally Accepted Accounting Principles (GAAP), for public and private companies and not-for-profit organizations.

It was established in 1973 as a successor to the Accounting Principles Board (APB). Its mission is to improve financial reporting and provide useful information to investors and other users of financial statements. The FASB operates under a transparent and inclusive due process system that involves stakeholders, such as investors, accountants, auditors, and regulators, in the standard-setting process.

Its activities include identifying emerging accounting and reporting issues, developing accounting and reporting standards, and interpreting and implementing existing standards. It also provides guidance and education to stakeholders on accounting and reporting matters through various forms of communication, such as publications, webcasts, and roundtable discussions.

The FASB's standards apply to financial statements that are prepared in accordance with GAAP. Its standards are considered authoritative and have a significant impact on financial reporting and the accounting profession.

GAAP (Generally Accepted Accounting Principles) A set of accounting rules, standards, and guidelines used to prepare and present financial statements for external users, such as investors, lenders, and regulators.

It provides a common language and framework for financial reporting, ensuring that financial information is accurate, consistent, and comparable across different organizations and industries. The principles are developed by various organizations, such as the Financial Accounting Standards Board (FASB) and the Securities and Exchange Commission (SEC) in the United States and are updated periodically to reflect changes in the accounting environment and the needs of users of financial statements.

Some of the key principles include the accrual basis of accounting, the matching principle, and the concept of materiality. The accrual basis of accounting requires that transactions be recorded when they occur, rather than when cash is received or paid. The matching principle requires that expenses be recorded in the same period as the revenue they helped to generate. Materiality requires that financial statements disclose all information that could influence a user's decision-making, but not every detail or trivial item.

GAAP is widely used in the United States and other countries, although some countries have their own accounting standards. It is important for businesses to follow GAAP in order to ensure that their financial statements are reliable, transparent, and useful to external users.

Goodwill An intangible asset on the balance sheet that represents the excess of the purchase price of a company over the fair market value of its identifiable net assets. In simpler terms, it is the amount that a company pays to acquire another company that is in excess of the fair market value of the acquired company's assets, liabilities, and equity.

It is recorded on the balance sheet as a long-term asset and is subject to annual impairment testing. If the fair value of the reporting unit that includes goodwill is less than its carrying amount, an impairment loss is recognized to write down the goodwill to its fair value.

Goodwill can be created in a variety of ways, such as through mergers and acquisitions, and it can represent a significant portion of a company's assets. However, investors should be aware that goodwill can be subjective and may be difficult to value accurately, which can lead to potential risks in investing in a company with a high value of goodwill on its balance sheet.

Income statement A financial statement that shows a business's revenues, expenses, and net income or loss over a period of time.

Inventory Goods held for sale or used in the production of goods for sale.

Liabilities Obligations or debts owed by a business or organization, such as loans or accounts payable.

Revenue Income earned by a business from the sale of goods or services.

Source and application of funds statement Shows the inflows and outflows of cash for a business or organization over a specific period of time. (See also **Sources of funds** and **Applications of funds**.) The statement is also known as the statement of changes in financial position, or cash flow statement.

It is useful in financial analysis and planning, as it can help businesses to forecast future cash flows and identify potential financial risks. By analyzing the sources and applications of funds over time, businesses can determine whether they are generating enough cash to support their operations and growth, and identify areas where cash may be constrained or excess.

Sources of funds The section of the source and application of funds statement that shows the various sources of cash inflows for the business during the period. It can include:

1. Operating activities, including cash generated from the business's day-to-day operations, such as sales revenue, collection of accounts receivable, and other income.

2. Investing activities, including cash generated from the sale or purchase of long-term assets, such as property, plant, and equipment, as well as from investments in other businesses.

3. Financing activities, including cash generated from borrowing activities, such as loans and bonds, as well as cash generated from equity financing activities, such as the sale of stocks or payment of dividends.

Trial balance A list of all the accounts in a company's general ledger and their balances, used to check the accuracy of the ledger.

ACKNOWLEDGEMENTS

I would like to acknowledge three people: Dr. Cundy, Charlie Ross, and David Friedenberg. Without them my life would have been significantly less interesting and enjoyable.

Although none of these men are alive today, they live on in my life and work and this book—an example of the immortality of mentorship. I benefit from their teachings and kindness every day, and so I share the value and joys of mentorship in the hopes of paying forward their investment in me in perpetuity.

DR. MARTIN CUNDY

Dr. Cundy was my earliest mentor, a brilliant Renaissance man who, when I was an eager fifteen-year-old, taught me Boolean algebra and immersed me in double negation, De Morgan's theorem, conjunction and disjunction. Dr. Cundy studied at Cambridge and was awarded the Smith's Prize for mathematics, the same prize the immortalized Alan Turing received there. (By some very strange coincidence, Alan Turing, considered one of the most brilliant mathematicians in the twentieth century, was also an alumni of Sherborne School, the boarding school I attended in Dorset, England.)

Dr. Cundy was a kind and generous man who took a stammering teen under his wing and opened his eyes to a world that most people never get to see. He taught me the unbelievable power of computers by showing me how our school teaching schedule could be reduced to a mathematical formula. He revealed how a rules-based system could simplify and compute the mindboggling complexity of an annual curriculum for 600 students with 46 classrooms, 55 teachers, and 5 grades for each scholastic year. He taught me how simple rules—such as "one teacher to a classroom," "chemistry must be taught in the chemistry lab," "only the right number of students should be assigned to each classroom"—could be programmed and then applied in seconds. He demonstrated to me that many problems people feel are impossible to solve can be answered with the knowledge of computing.

Dr. Cundy also showed me that kindness and caring were key ingredients in teaching. My toast with marmalade had finally fallen with the marmalade-side up.

CHARLIE ROSS

Charlie Ross was a genuine visionary light years ahead of his time. In 1967 I was lucky enough to join his company, which he had presciently named International Data Highways (IDH).

In order to join Charlie's group you needed to take and pass a full day of testing held in the massive ballroom of the Russell Hotel in London. I'll never forget it. Hundreds of desks were lined up in neat rows, filled with people from all walks of life. It was akin to a Broadway open call: no qualifications needed, just turn up ready to write eight hours of exams.

Out of the hundreds of applicants, only eight would be chosen. I was among those eight and so got to meet one the most interesting people of my life.

For some reason Charlie took me under his wing (maybe he saw a younger kindred spirit). I was the only employee who he would meet with regularly to expound on his next vision. He would give me very complex problems to solve in the nascent world of real-time computing. Day by day, he increased my confidence and encouraged me to dream about capabilities that everyone else said were impossible. He encouraged me to be creative and lit a spark inside me that still burns today.

Charlie was the first dreamer I'd ever met, and I think about him often. I still hear his raucous laughter as we worked together on his perpetual dream machine.

DAVID FRIEDENBERG

David Friedenberg (you read about him earlier in the book) was the senior banker in a bank called Seattle First National Bank, his corner desk overlooking the vast pool of bankers on the building's first floor. Seafirst, as it was known, had about 70% of the local banking business and was the most important bank in the northwest United States at the time. Dave took me from relative obscurity and gave me the opportunity to turn around some of his most important customers.

Dave had moved from New York to Seattle in the early 1970s, landing in a city where businesses were experiencing extraordinary hardship after Boeing laid off more than 50,000 people. A commanding presence, Dave was fair but expected complete honesty from his customers, especially when it came to their financial affairs.

Dave adopted me immediately after my arrival, seeing in me the potential to successfully work with his customers who were experiencing financial hardships. Without Dave this book would not have been written. I owe so much to him for giving me, a twenty-seven-year-old with no qualifications, a conveyer belt of opportunities for seventeen years. He taught me the value of complete transparency in the face of dauntingly challenging financial situations. He taught me how to put out the fire instead of running away from it. His faith in me has lasted a lifetime and gave me the strength to face my own difficult situations.

These three gentlemen provided me with vision, confidence, and the permission to dream. My obligation is to pass it forward in as many ways as I can.

INDEX

fraudulent accounting of, 179

importance of accurate valuation
of, 179

LIFO (last in, first out), 178

overvaluation of, 178, 181

overview of, 48

physical count of, 176–177

physical storage of, 176

raw materials, 177, 179

valuation variations in, 175

work in progress (WIP), 177,
178, 179

write-down of, 178

investors. *See* banks and investors

ISO 9000, 158

J

Jeremiahs. *See* employees:
naysayers

K

kickbacks. *See* business assessment

Kübler-Ross, Elisabeth, 12

L

leadership

accountability of, 54

collaboration fostered by, 53, 55

confidence modelled by,
55, 56, 60

externally sourced for
turnaround, 56–57

forward mindset of, 55

and honesty, 42, 46, 55, 133

at meetings, 91

observational skills of, 59–61

overview of in turnaround
process, 41–42

personable approach by, 56–57

positive future tone set by,
53, 54–55, 56

responsive, 95–96, 96–97

role in clean-up process, 121

sensitivity in, 51–52

trust in, 54, 54–55, 57–58

values modelled by, 62–64

See also communication;
eliminating constraints;
mentorship; stewardship

Litton Industries, 2–3

loans. *See* banks and investors

London Stock Exchange, 22

M

management (existing)

challenges of in turnaround, 51

meeting with, 41, 51–52

need for observation of, 59–61

See also leadership; stewardship

*Marmion: A Tale of Flodden
Field*, 175

McMurtry, Sir David, 190

meetings

attendee mix at, 89

benefits of, 87

benefits of short, 56

with CFO, 53, 65–67

as employee engagement tool, 95

with existing leadership, 41,
51–52

under the go-forward plan,
193–194

with longest-tenured
employee(s), 53, 67–68

as observational opportunity,
90–91

ABOUT THE AUTHOR

Mike Dunlop was born in Cornwall, England, in 1947. He left school at age eighteen and began his career at a company with a prescient name, International Data Highways. There he learned about the wonders of computing under his mentor Charlie Ross, who would have a profound impact on his life and his career.

In 1973, with Britain in deep economic trouble, Mike emigrated to the US and began work at a division of a large conglomerate called Litton Industries. He was dismissed in his first year. But it turned out to be a lucky break.

After being fired, Mike launched his first company, a computer consulting firm that advised small- and medium-size companies who were buying their first computers.

While working with one of these companies, Mike spotted his first opportunity to turn around a company in financial trouble. This led to him turning around another thirty-three companies over the next seventeen years. The inspiration for this book came from his learnings during those years.

Mike has a long record of buying companies and making them profitable. In 1984, he acquired two businesses in Europe. Both were in financial trouble, and Mike's background helped him to turn these companies into profitable assets.

In 1986, he purchased an aerospace manufacturing company in Portland, Oregon, called Zirca-Tech. He changed the name to QPM Aerospace, and under his management, QPM's revenues grew from $1 million to $40 million in the following ten years. After the 9/11 terrorist attack, sales dropped 30% but recovered three years later.

In 1998, Mike designed a software system called Net-Inspect to improve quality in aerospace manufacturing plants. The software worked so well that it was spun off into a separate company and became one of the first SaaS (software as a service) systems worldwide. Twenty-six years later, Net-Inspect has become the most widely used aerospace quality software in the world with over eight thousand companies in fifty-six countries operating on this platform.

In 2011, Mike sold QPM to focus on Net-Inspect.

Always the entrepreneur, Mike started a new company in 2022 called Autonomous Machining to fully automate the manufacturing process for aerospace components.

Mike lives in Seattle, Washington. He's an experienced public speaker, and he offers his wisdom and stories on a weekly podcast, available on Spotify and YouTube.